KitchenAid
Ice Cream Maker
Cookbook

By

Elizabeth Marie Puckett

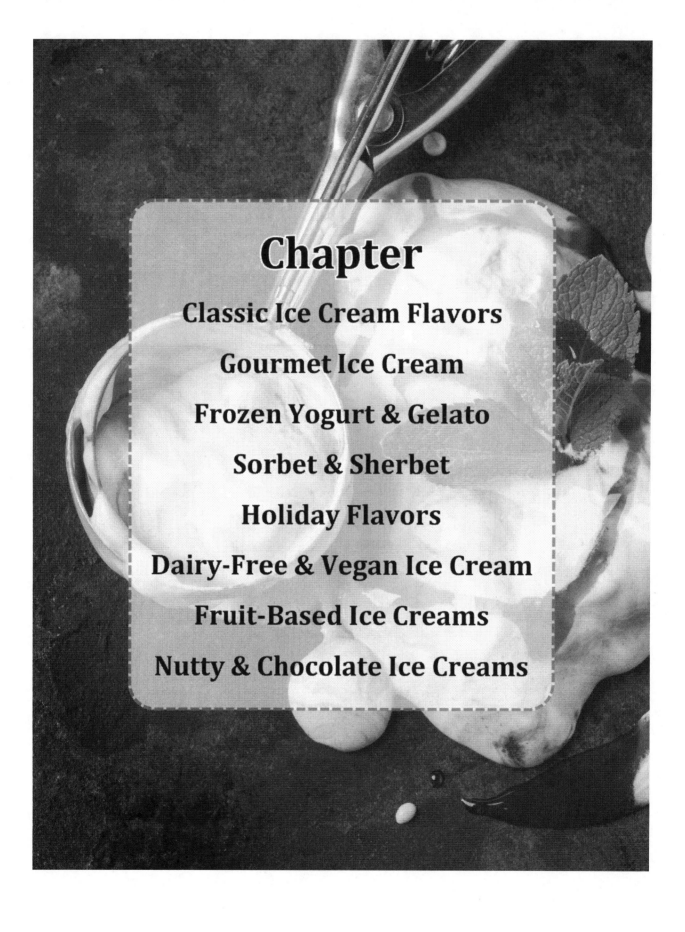

Chapter

Classic Ice Cream Flavors

Gourmet Ice Cream

Frozen Yogurt & Gelato

Sorbet & Sherbet

Holiday Flavors

Dairy-Free & Vegan Ice Cream

Fruit-Based Ice Creams

Nutty & Chocolate Ice Creams

Classic Ice Cream Flavors

Gourmet Ice Cream

Frozen Yogurt & Gelato

Sorbet & Sherbet

Holiday Flavors

Dairy-Free & Vegan Ice Cream

Fruit-Based Ice Creams

Nutty & Chocolate Ice Creams

TABLE OF CONTENT

Introduction:

Welcome to the KitchenAid Ice Cream Maker Cookbook, where you can find frozen treats different from those you're used to. This book will help you enjoy 100 tasty frozen treats suitable for all tastes and dietary needs, no matter how much you know about them or how interested you are in them.

You'll find traditional and new flavours in this cookbook, from the classic appeal of vanilla and chocolate to the sophisticated appeal of gourmet creations. Whether you want the rich, creamy texture of gelato, the cool, sour taste of sorbet, or the sweet, holiday-themed ice creams, these recipes will quickly become your go-to favourites. For people who want to eat healthier, our dairy-free and vegan options taste just like regular ice cream but don't make you feel bad. We also put in a range of fruit-based ice creams and nutty treats so everyone can find something they like.

Every recipe has been carefully designed to work perfectly with your KitchenAid Ice Cream Maker. Making these frozen treats is just as much fun as eating them. This cookbook will give you the information and ideas you need to make every scoop memorable, whether making a quick batch for a daily treat or a show-stopping dessert for a special event.

Get your ice cream maker and ingredients ready, and get ready to discover the wonderful world of making your frozen treats. With these 100 delicious recipes, you'll be well on your way to becoming an ice cream master and wowing your family and friends with your tasty creations. Let's jump right in and make some frozen magic!

Ice Cream Making Tips

Here are some essential ice cream-making tips to help you achieve the perfect frozen dessert every time:

1. Work with good ingredients

Your ingredients have much to do with how good your ice cream tastes. To make sure your ice cream tastes great, use fresh cream, good vanilla extract, and ripe fruits.

2. Make your base cold

Make sure your ice cream base is very cold before you start churning. This speeds up the freezing process and makes the ice cream smoother and creamier.

3. Don't put too much in the machine

When you use your KitchenAid ice cream maker, don't put too much in it. Since ice cream expands when it freezes, filling the bowl only two-thirds of the way to the top will let it do that and improve the consistency.

4. Use the right mix-ins at the right time

Add chocolate chips, nuts, or fruit at the end after a few minutes of rolling. In this way, they don't sink to the bottom or get too crushed.

5. Freeze the bowl ahead of time

Before you start, make sure the bowl of your KitchenAid Ice Cream Maker is quite frozen. This takes about 15 to 24 hours in a freezer, so plan ahead. To get the right texture, you need a well-frozen bowl.

6. Do not rush the process of churning

Don't rush the churning process; let the machine do its job. When you churn ice cream the right way, you add air to the mixture, which makes it light and creamy.

7. Store it right

Put the ice cream in a container that won't let air in. Finally, cover the ice cream with parchment paper or plastic wrap and close the container. Crystals in your ice cream will spoil it quickly.

8. Try out different flavours

Feel free to think outside the box! Try different flavour combinations, add-ins, and sweeteners to make ice cream that tastes just right for you.

9. Let it get hard.

Your ice cream will be soft-serve after you churn it. Freeze it for three to four hours before serving to make it firmer. This hardening phase helps the ice cream set and makes it taste better.

10. Put it out at the right temperature

Before you scoop, let your ice cream sit at room temperature for a few minutes. This makes it easier to serve and brings out all of its flavor.

After reading these tips, you should be able to make ice cream that tastes just as good as any store-bought kind. Have fun churning!

How To Clean KitchenAid Ice Cream Maker?

Follow these steps to clean your KitchenAid ice cream maker and keep it in great shape for next time:

1. Detach the Bowl and Other Parts:

Carefully take the mixer's freezer bowl, dasher (paddle), and any other parts away.

2. Clean the Freezer Bowl Gently:

Use warm water & a soft cloth or sponge to rinse the freezer bowl. Do not put it in hot water or use hot water, as sudden changes in temperature could hurt the freezing gel inside. You should never put it in the dishwasher.

3. Wash the Dasher and Other Parts:

The dash, drive assembly, and other parts can usually be washed in the dishwasher (check the manual for your model). If you wash by hand, use warm, soapy water and a good rinse.

4. Dry Completely:

Let the freezer bowl and all of its parts dry entirely in the air before putting them back in the freezer until the next time you need them. If there is moisture in the bowl, ice crystals could form, changing the texture of your ice cream.

5. Store Carefully:

If you can, put the freezer bowl in a plastic bag & put it in the freezer. This prevents freezer smells from changing the taste of your ice cream.

If you do these things, your KitchenAid Ice Cream Maker will stay clean and ready to use whenever you want to make tasty frozen treats.

Ice Cream Healthy Benefits

When eaten in moderation and made with good ingredients, ice cream can be good for you in surprising ways:

1. Source of Important Nutrients:
Milk, which is in ice cream, gives you calcium, vitamin D, and phosphorus. For strong bones and teeth, you need these nutrients.

2. Good Source of Protein:
A small ice cream cone can provide protein, which is important for building muscle and keeping your body healthy.

3. Energy Boost:
Ice cream is a tasty treat that is high in carbs and makes you feel full quickly. It does have sugar, so you should only eat small amounts of it, but it can charge you up.

4. Mood-Boosting Effects:
Eating ice cream can release serotonin, a hormone that makes you feel better. Having a favorite flavor can also improve your mood and lower your stress.

5. Some Types of Ice Cream Have Live Probiotics:
Some ice creams, especially those that say "frozen yogurt," have live probiotics that help keep your gut healthy and your immune system strong.

6. Special diets can choose dairy-free options:
Vegan and dairy-free ice creams made with almond, coconut, or oat milk are suitable for people who have to watch what they eat and still have healthy fats, fiber, and vitamins.!

7. Carotenoids in ice creams with fruit:

Berry or mango sorbets, for example, contain natural antioxidants from real fruit that fight free radicals and are suitable for your health in general.

Due to its high sugar & fat content, ice cream should still be eaten only occasionally. However, if you make smart choices and watch your portions, you can enjoy it as part of a healthy diet

1. VANILLA BEAN ICE CREAM

Prep Time: 45 Minutes | Cook Time: 40 Minutes

Total Time: 1 Hour 25 Minutes | Serving: 4

Ingredients

- 1/2 cup of brown sugar
- 1 vanilla bean
- 1/3 cup of milk
- 4 egg yolks
- strawberry sauce
- 1 3/4 cup of heavy cream

Instructions

1. Boil the milk in a small pot or saucepan and let it cool. Cut the vanilla bean down the middle and use a knife or a tsp to scrape the seeds.
2. Mix the sugar, egg yolks, vanilla bean, and seeds into the cooled milk. Stirring occasionally, cook over slow heat for about 15 minutes or until it thickens. Remove from heat and let cool. Take the vanilla bean out of the mix.
3. Whip the cream, then slowly fold it into the vanilla mixture. For ice cream, put it in the bowl and start churning it. The ice cream should be ready in 30 minutes, but check it every few minutes until it's done. It needs to be thick but not hard. Cover the ice cream with a dish and freeze it for about two hours. It tastes good with strawberry sauce. Enjoy!

2. CHOCOLATE FUDGE BROWNIE ICE CREAM

Prep Time: 20 Minutes | Cook Time: 00 Minutes

Total Time: 20 Minutes | Serving: 8

Ingredients

- 2 cups of heavy cream
- 1 cup of chopped brownies
- 5 egg yolks
- 1/2 tsp vanilla
- 1/4 cup of cocoa powder
- 1/4 cup of hot fudge sauce
- 1/4 tsp salt
- 1 cup of whole milk
- 4 ounce semi sweet chocolate
- 3/4 cup of sugar

Instructions

1. Mix the cocoa powder, sugar, salt, heavy cream, and milk in a large saucepan.
2. Mix it up and heat it on medium-high until it starts to bubble. Add the chocolate that isn't too sweet. Mix until it's smooth.
3. Whisk the egg yolks in a different bowl.
4. Slowly pour half of the chocolate cream mixture into the egg yolks while whisking them very hard.
5. Add another 1 cup of the chocolate cream mixture as you whisk, half a cup at a time.
6. Place the egg mix back into the saucepan and heat it for five minutes or until it thickens.
7. Add the vanilla extract and mix well.
8. Put it back in the bowl.
9. For ten minutes, put the bowl in a bath of ice water and stir it every so often.
10. To cool it down, put the bowl in the fridge with the lid on for 30 minutes to an hour.
11. After setting up the ice cream maker, pour the mix into it and let it run according to the instructions that came with it.
12. 3Sprinkle your brownie pieces on top in the last five minutes.
13. Put half of the ice cream into a 9x5-inch loaf pan. Then, drizzle with half of the hot fudge and mix it all. Do it again with the rest of the hot fudge and ice cream.
14. Put the dish in the freezer with the lid on for another 6 hours or overnight to completely freeze it.

3. STRAWBERRY ICE CREAM

Prep Time: 25 Minutes | Cook Time: 30 Minutes

Total Time: 55 Minutes | Serving: 8

Ingredients

- 4 large egg yolks
- ½ cup of granulated sugar
- 2 Tbsp Watkins vanilla
- 1 pound fresh strawberries
- 1½ cups of whole milk
- 1 cup of granulated sugar
- 1½ cups of heavy cream

Instructions

1. Get strawberries ready. Take cold water and run it over the strawberries. Peel and cut them up, then put them in a bowl. After that, add 1/2 cup of sugar and mix it in. Leave the strawberries on your counter for about an hour so juices can form.
2. Make strawberry puree. Put the strawberries and juices into a blender. Pulse until the mixture is very smooth. Put the puree into a large bowl or an 8-cup of measuring cup.
3. Warm up eggs. Mix the egg yolks & half cup of sugar in a bowl. To get the milk to 165 degrees, put it in a saucepan over medium-low heat.
4. Whisk the eggs all the time as you add 1/2 cup of hot milk at a time. After that, add the egg mix to the pan and heat it to 165 degrees.
5. Add the rest of the ingredients. After letting it cool a bit, add it to the big bowl. After that, add the vanilla extract, heavy cream, and the rest of the sugar. Mix well.
6. Relax. Put the liquid mixture in the fridge for at least four hours with the plastic wrap on top. The mix needs to be very cold!
7. Make ice cream. Put the chilled ice cream mix into the bowl of your 2-quart ice cream maker and turn it on. Stir the ice cream with the mixer for a while until it sets.
8. It will get thicker and rise to the top of the bowl. The mixer might move a little more slowly.
9. Put it away. The container must be put in the freezer to set up even more. At first, the ice cream will be very soft. Freezing it for a few hours helps it get firm.
10. Do it. If you want, serve the ice cream with some extra fresh strawberries!

4. MINT CHOCOLATE CHIP ICE CREAM

Prep Time: 5 Minutes | Cook Time: 15 Minutes

Total Time: 20 Minutes | Serving: 8

Ingredients

- 1½ cups of whole milk
- 1½ cups of heavy whipping cream
- 4 egg yolks
- 100 grams of dark chocolate
- ¾-1 cup of granulated sugar
- 1 tbsp vanilla extract
- 1 tsp pure mint extract
- green food coloring

Instructions

1. Follow the directions on how to freeze the ice cream maker bowl.
2. Mix the cream, milk, sugar, and egg yolks in a large saucepan using an electric whisk until the mixture is smooth.
3. Set the pan on medium warm and stir until it gets thick. It's not going to get thick like pudding, but it will. Add the mint and vanilla and mix well.
4. Put it in a big bowl or measuring cup made of glass. Put a piece of plastic wrap on top to keep skin from forming.
5. Put in the fridge until it's freezing.
6. Put it in the ice cream maker and churn it for 20 minutes or until it's the consistency of soft serve. You can stir the chocolate at the end or add it in the last 5 minutes of churning.
7. Put the mixture into a baking dish or glass loaf pan and freeze for 4 to 6 hours or until it is firm.
8. Let it sit for 5 to 10 minutes at room temperature before serving. Wrap extra food in plastic wrap and freeze for up to three months.

5. BUTTER PECAN ICE CREAM

Prep Time: 5 Minutes | Cook Time: 20 Minutes | Total Time: 25 Minutes | Serving: 16

Ingredients
- 1 tbsp butter
- 2 large eggs
- ½ cup of heavy cream
- 1 ½ cups of half-and-half cream
- ⅓ cup of chopped pecans
- 1 tsp vanilla extract
- 1 cup of brown sugar

Instructions
1. Warm up some butter in a small pan over medium-low heat. For 3 to 5 minutes, stir pecans in hot butter until they are lightly browned and smell good. Put away.
2. In a large bowl, beat the eggs together. Set this bowl aside.
3. In a saucepan, mix half-and-half and brown sugar well. Heat until it starts to boil, then take it off the heat. Slowly put the hot mixture into the eggs while whisking all the time. Bring the custard back to the saucepan and stir it around a few times to make it thick enough to coat the back of a spoon. When you can see a clear line when you run your finger down the back of the coated spoon, the custard mix is ready. Take it off the heat and add the vanilla, cream, and pecans.
4. Put it in an ice cream maker and freeze it the way the machine says to.

6. COFFEE ICE CREAM

Prep Time: 25 Minutes | Cook Time: 10 Minutes | Total Time: 35 Minutes | Serving: 5

Ingredients
- ⅛ tsp salt
- 2 ¼ cups of heavy cream
- 1 ½ tsp vanilla extract
- 6 egg yolks
- 1 ½ cups of granulated sugar
- 2 ½ cups of whole milk
- 2 tbsp coffee granules

Instructions
1. Put the coffee grounds, milk, sugar, and salt in a medium-sized saucepan. Over medium heat, stir the food until it starts to steam. Bring down the heat.
2. In a bowl, beat the egg yolks just a little. Slowly put half of the hot milk into the eggs while whisking them all the time. Put the mixture back in the pot and cook it over medium heat, stirring it now and then for about 5 minutes or until it gets thick.
3. Put a fine-mesh sieve over a medium-sized bowl and pour the custard. Leave space between the plastic wrap and the custard's surface so the skin doesn't form. Put in the fridge until cold.
4. Add the cream and vanilla to the custard and mix them until smooth before making the ice cream. To get the ice cream maker to churn, do what it says.
5. You can eat it immediately or put it in a container that you can freeze. The ice cream can stay frozen for up to two weeks.

7. CARAMEL ICE CREAM

Prep Time: 25 Minutes | Cook Time: 25 Minutes

Total Time: 50 Minutes | Serving: 10

Ingredients
- 2 cups of heavy whipping cream
- 1 cup of granulated sugar
- 1 cup of milk

Instructions

1. You can get one here if you don't have one.
2. Put sugar in a big, heavy pot.
3. Over medium-low heat, stir the sugar until it melts and turns a golden brown.
4. Take it off the heat.
5. Be careful as you add milk to the sugar that has turned caramelized.
6. Watch out because the sugar will harden, and the mixture will splash. Do not worry!
7. Over low heat, stir the mixture until it's smooth again.
8. Put the whipped cream and stir until it's smooth and well-mixed.
9. Take it off the heat and let it cool down.
10. Put the mix in the fridge for at least three hours after it's fantastic.
11. Put the chilled mixture into the machine that makes ice cream.
12. Mix for about 25 to 30 minutes or as the manufacturer directs.
13. Enjoy! If you want, serve with toppings!

8. CLASSIC LEMON ICE CREAM

Prep Time: 30 Minutes | Cook Time: 00 Minutes

Total Time: 30 Minutes | Serving: 8

Ingredients
- pinch of salt
- 1 cup of sugar
- 3 tbsp finely grated lemon zest
- 2 cups of heavy cream
- ½ cup of freshly squeezed lemon juice

Instructions

1. Mix the heavy cream, sugar, and salt in a bowl. Put the bowl in the fridge while you peel and squeeze the lemons. Get it out of the refrigerator and mix the sugar with a whisk.
2. Mix the lemon juice and zest with a whisk. After putting the mixture in the fridge or freezer for at least an hour, cover it and chill it until it's freezing.
3. Follow the steps that came with your ice cream maker to churn. When it's thick, like soft serve, put it in a container, cover it, and freeze it until it's solid. This could take a few hours or all night.
4. Serve with a scoop.

9. OREGANO ICE CREAM

Prep Time: 15 Minutes | Cook Time: 25 Minutes

Total Time: 40 Minutes | Serving: 10

Ingredients

- Honey dark
- 1 cup of milk
- ½ cup of oregano leaves
- 2 cups of heavy whipping cream
- ½ cup of sugar

Instructions

1. Put the milk, cream, and sugar into a saucepan and heat them until they bubble.
2. Take it off the heat, add the oregano, and cover it.
3. After adding the milk, let the oregano soak for about three hours.
4. Take the oregano leaves out of the milk mixture and throw them away.
5. Cool the milk mix in the fridge for about two hours.
6. For 25 to 30 minutes, or as long as the maker says, churn the mixture in an ice cream maker.
7. Sprinkle honey on the ice cream, and you're ready to serve. If you want, you can decorate with fresh oregano leaves.

10. EGGNOG ICE CREAM

Prep Time: 45 Minutes | Cook Time: 00 Minutes

Total Time: 45 Minutes | Serving: 10

Ingredients

- 1 can sweetened condensed milk
- 1 tsp vanilla extract
- 2 cups of eggnog
- 2 cups of heavy cream

Instructions

1. Mix the heavy cream, coconut milk, eggnog, and vanilla in a large bowl. Follow the manufacturer's instructions and freeze the mixture until it has a "soft-serve" consistency.
2. Add the ice cream into a plastic container with a lid that holds 1 or 2 quarts. Cover the top with plastic wrap & seal the container. If you want the best ice cream, leave it in the freezer for at least two hours or overnight.

11. BUTTERSCOTCH ICE CREAM

Prep Time: 20 Minutes | Cook Time: 25 Minutes

Total Time: 45 Minutes | Serving: 10

Ingredients
- 1 cup of milk
- 2 tbsp butter
- 2 cups of heavy whipping cream
- 2 tsp vanilla extract
- 1 cup of brown sugar

Instructions
1. Mix sugar, vanilla, and butter in a large saucepan.
2. Put the mixture on medium heat and heat it until it starts to bubble.
3. Put half a cup of milk and stir it in again and again until it's smooth.
4. Take it off the heat.
5. Mix well with the heavy whipping cream and the rest of the milk. Cool.
6. Put it in the fridge for at least three hours.
7. Put the butterscotch mixture that has been chilled into your ice cream maker.
8. For about 25 to 30 minutes, or as long as the maker says, mix in an ice cream maker.
9. Enjoy! Feel free to add toppings if you want!

12. COOKIES AND CREAM ICE CREAM

Prep Time: 10 Minutes | Cook Time: 30 Minutes

Total Time: 40 Minutes | Serving: 8

Ingredients
- 1 1/2 Tbsp pure vanilla
- 1 1/2 cups of whole milk
- 1 1/2 cups of half and half cream
- 1/4 tsp salt
- 12 cookies crushed
- 1 1/2 cups of sugar
- 1 1/2 cups of whipping cream

Instructions
1. Mix everything except the cookies, then pour it into the ice cream maker.
2. Follow the directions given by the manufacturer.
3. Mix the cookies in the last five minutes of processing with the ice cream.
4. Freeze ice cream in a container with insulation until it is firm.

13. LAVENDER ICE CREAM

Prep Time: 30 Minutes | Cook Time: 15 Minutes

Total Time: 45 Minutes | Serving: 4

Ingredients

- 2 cups of heavy whipping cream
- ⅛ tsp salt
- ⅔ cup of honey
- 1 cup of half-and-half
- 2 tbsp dried lavender flowers
- 2 eggs

Instructions

1. In a heavy 2-quart saucepan, heat the heavy cream, half-and-half, honey, and lavender flowers. Stir the mixture every so often until the cream just starts to bubble. Take it off the heat and cover it. Let it sit for 30 minutes.
2. Using a fine-mesh sieve, pour the cream mixture into a bowl. Throw away the lavender flowers. Pour the strained cream mixture back into a clean saucepan. Put it on medium heat and wait about 5 minutes until it gets hot.
3. Put the eggs and salt in a bowl and mix them. Slowly put in 1 cup of hot cream while whisking.
4. Add the egg mix to the saucepan's remaining hot cream. Over medium-low heat, stir the custard all the time with a wooden spoon for about 5 minutes, or until it coats the back of the spoon and an instant-read thermometer reads 175 degrees F.
5. Using a fine-mesh sieve, pour the custard into a bowl. Allow to cool completely, stirring now and then, for about 15 minutes. Cover and let it sit for at least three hours.
6. Follow the steps on the ice cream maker to freeze the custard for about 20 minutes. Put the mixture in a container that won't let air in and freeze it to harden.

14. MATCHA GREEN TEA ICE CREAM

Prep Time: 10 Minutes | Cook Time: 10 Minutes

Total Time: 20 Minutes | Serving: 8

Ingredients

- 1 cup of whole milk
- 1 tbsp matcha green tea powder
- 2 cups of heavy whipping cream
- ¾ cup of white sugar
- 2 eggs

Instructions

1. In a bowl, whisk matcha powder to get rid of any lumps. Mix a little milk with a whisk until all the matcha powder is gone. Put the rest of the milk slowly while whisking.
2. Move the matcha mix to a pot. Put the cream and cook over medium-low heat, stirring now and then, for about 5 minutes or until everything is hot.
3. In a bowl, mix sugar and eggs with an electric whisk. Add 1/2 cup of the hot matcha mixture to the egg mixture and quickly whisk until everything is well mixed. Do it again with the rest of the matcha mixture. Put the mix back into the pot.
4. Mix the matcha over medium-low heat and stir it around for about three minutes or until it's fully heated. Once it's cool enough, take it off the heat and let it sit there for 20 minutes. Put in the fridge for at least 4 hours to get cold.
5. Put the chilled matcha mixture into an ice cream maker and freeze it for about 20 minutes, or as the manufacturer directs. Put in a container that won't let air in and freeze for about 4 hours or until firm.

15. BOURBON VANILLA BEAN ICE CREAM

Prep Time: 15 Minutes | Cook Time: 15 Minutes

Total Time: 30 Minutes | Serving: 16

Ingredients

- 1 cup of whole milk
- ⅛ tsp coarse Kosher salt
- 2 cups of cold heavy whipping cream
- 1 tbsp good-quality bourbon
- 1 vanilla bean
- ¾ cup of dark brown sugar
- 5 large egg yolks

Instructions

1. Mix the egg yolks and brown sugar with a whisk in a large saucepan until smooth. Add the salt, milk, and 1 cup of cream and mix them with a whisk.
2. To make the custard, put it in a pan over medium-low heat and stir it with a spatula until it bubbles and steam. Do not let it boil.
3. Take it off the heat and strain the custard through a mesh sieve to eliminate any egg bits. Cover and chill in the fridge until very cold, preferably overnight, to let the flavours come together.

4. Whip the last cup of cream with an electric mixer until soft peaks form. Add the whipped cream to the custard that has been chilled and mix it well.
5. Follow the directions in the ice cream maker's manual to churn the custard. Add the bourbon in the last minute of churning. Put the mix in a container that can hold ice cream and cover it. Freeze it for 8 to 10 hours, or until it gets firm.

16. WHITE CHOCOLATE AND RASPBERRY ICE CREAM

Prep Time: 10 Minutes | Cook Time: 20 Minutes

Total Time: 30 Minutes | Serving: 12

Ingredients

- 2 cups of heavy whipping cream
- 5 egg yolks
- 1 vanilla bean
- 1 package of white chocolate chips
- 1 package frozen raspberries
- 1 tsp vanilla extract
- 1 pinch salt
- 1 cup of whole milk
- ¾ cup of white sugar

Instructions

1. Use medium-low heat to warm the milk, sugar, vanilla beans, seeds, and salt in a saucepan. This should take about 5 minutes.
2. Whisk together egg yolks and about a cup of the hot milk in a bowl. Mix the egg mixture into a saucepan. Stir the custard often for another 5 to 7 minutes or until it gets thick enough to coat the back of a spoon. Take out the vanilla bean.
3. The custard will melt if you stir white chocolate chips into it. Empty the custard into a big bowl. Put the heavy cream and vanilla extract and mix them. Cover and put in the fridge until it's cold.
4. Put the chilled mixture into an ice cream maker. Follow the maker's instructions for freezing until the texture of "soft-serve" is reached. Freeze the ice cream while you cook the raspberries.
5. In a saucepan, warm the raspberries over medium to low heat for 7-10 minutes or until the raspberries start to break up. Put raspberries through a sieve set over a bowl to remove the seeds. Throw away the seeds.
6. Mix raspberries slowly into soft ice cream to make ribbons out of them. Put the ice cream in a plastic jar with a lid that can hold one or two quarts. Wrap the lid in plastic wrap and close the jar. The best ice cream is made after being frozen for at least two hours or all night.

17. PISTACHIO ICE CREAM WITH ROSEWATER

Prep Time: 20 Minutes | Cook Time: 00 Minutes

Total Time: 20 Minutes | Serving: 6

Ingredients

- ½ cup of granulated sugar
- 1 ⅓ cups of whole milk
- ½ tsp ground cardamom
- 2 Tbsp light corn syrup
- ½ tsp saffron
- 2 Tbsp dry milk powder
- 1 ⅓ cups of heavy cream
- ½ cup of Sweet Pistachio cream
- ¼ tsp xanthan gum
- 3 tsp rosewater

For garnish:

- dried edible roses
- ⅓ cup of unsalted roasted pistachios

Instructions

1. Put the sugar, dry milk, saffron, ground cardamom, and xanthan gum in a small bowl and mix them well.
2. Pour the corn syrup into a medium-sized pot set over medium-low heat. Then, stir in the whole milk. When you add the sugar mixture and the sweet pistachio cream, whisk it very hard until it is smooth. Stir the mixture often and change the heat to keep it from simmering for about three minutes or until the sugar is completely dissolved. Take the pot off the heat.
3. Rose water and cream should be added. Mix everything with a whisk. Use a fine-mesh sieve to pour the custard into the bowl.
4. Put the mixture in a container that won't let air in. Cover it and put it in the fridge for at least 6 or 24 hours for better texture and flavor. While it's resting, stir the base back together if it starts to separate.
5. Then, put the mix into an ice cream maker and turn it on. Only churn the mixture until it feels like a soft serve.
6. Quickly put the ice cream into a container that can go in the freezer.
7. Put parchment paper on the ice cream and press it down so it sticks. Then, put a lid on top of that. The parchment can hang over the edge. At least 6 hours should pass between putting it in the freezer and becoming firm. It can last up to three months.
8. To finish, add more sweet pistachio cream and crushed dried roses that can be eaten.

18. ESPRESSO CHOCOLATE CHIP ICE CREAM

Prep Time: 10 Minutes | Cook Time: 20 Minutes

Total Time: 30 Minutes | Serving: 8

Ingredients

- ½ cup of mini chocolate chips
- 2-3 tbsp espresso powder
- 2 cups of heavy cream
- 7 ounce sweetened condensed milk

Instructions

1. For 24 hours, put your ice cream maker bowl in the freezer.
2. Cream, condensed milk, and espresso powder should all be mixed in a large size bowl using a whisk.
3. Put the ingredients into the ice cream maker's bowl, then freeze the ice cream overnight, following the maker's directions.
4. Add the chocolate chips about halfway through the process.
5. It only took me about 20 minutes to churn the ice cream. Once it's done, put it in a bowl that can go in the freezer and freeze it for at least 4 hours.

19. BLACK SESAME ICE CREAM

Prep Time: 15 Minutes | Cook Time: 10 Minutes

Total Time: 25 Minutes | Serving: 8

Ingredients

- 100 ml whipping/heavy cream
- 5 egg yolks organic
- 75 g Japanese black sesame paste
- 110 g sugar
- pinch salt Fleur de sel
- 500 ml whole milk full-fat

Instructions

1. Start up Sesame.
2. Suppose you want to use whole seeds; dry roast black sesame seeds in a nonstick pan for four to five minutes. Then, use a coffee grinder to grind them up.
3. Use black sesame paste that has already been packaged instead.
4. Warm the milk slowly in a saucepan with a heavy bottom.
5. In a large bowl with a lid, beat the egg yolks & sugar together until they are smooth. Mix the salt and black sesame powder in with a whisk until the mixture is smooth.
6. Add half the hot milk to the black sesame mixture and mix it with a whisk. Then, return the mixture to the saucepan. Keep whisking the mixture to keep it smooth, and heat it over medium-low heat until it gets a little thicker. Take it off the heat right away so the eggs don't curdle. When done, the mixture should be smooth enough to coat a spoon.
7. After adding the cold cream, let it cool down. Then, cover it and put it in the fridge for at least two hours or overnight.

8. Follow the directions in the ice cream maker's manual to churn the mixture. Then, freeze it for at least an hour before serving.

20. MAPLE PECAN ICE CREAM

Prep Time: 30 Minutes | Cook Time: 15 Minutes

Total Time: 45 Minutes | Serving: 8

Ingredients

- ➢ 2 cups of whipping cream
- ➢ a pinch of salt
- ➢ 2 large eggs
- ➢ 1/2 cup of chopped pecans
- ➢ 1 cup of coffee cream
- ➢ 1 cup of maple syrup

Instructions

1. In a medium sized saucepan, bring the maple syrup to a boil. Take it off the heat and let it simmer for about 5 minutes or until the maple syrup is almost gone.
2. Add the creams and salt and mix well. Bring the mix to a boil, then take it off the heat.
3. Mix the eggs in a small bowl. Slowly put about a cup of the hot mixture while mixing. Mix this with the hot cream in the saucepan, then whisk it together.
4. Keep whisking the mixture while cooking on medium heat until it gets hot. Don't let it get too hot.
5. Put the mix into a glass bowl. Cover and put in the fridge for three to four hours or until it's cold.
6. Follow the directions on the package to freeze the mixture, and add the pecans 30 minutes before it's done.
7. Put it in a container that won't let air in, and freeze it overnight.

21. EARL GREY ICE CREAM

Prep Time: 5 Minutes | Cook Time: 15 Minutes

Total Time: 20 Minutes | Serving: 5

Ingredients

- 3/4 cup of sugar
- 1 cup of whole milk
- 5 egg yolks
- 2 cups of half and half
- 6 Earl Grey tea bags
- 1 tsp. vanilla extract

Instructions

1. Warm the milk, half-and-half, and sugar in a small saucepan over medium-low heat, stirring now and then. Take the pan off the heat when the milk starts to steam. Cover the pan & let the tea steep at room temperature for 15-20 minutes, stirring now and then. Take out the tea bags and stir the tea again.
2. Whisk the egg yolks & vanilla together in a different bowl until they become foamy. Once the milk mixture is warm again, quickly whisk in two tbsp of the hot milk mixture into the eggs until they are well mixed. Do this two or three more times with more of the milk mixture. TThen, beat the egg yolks quickly with a whisk while slowly adding the rest of the milk mixture.
3. Add the new milk and eggs to the saucepan again. Scrub and stir the bottom of the pan often while cooking over medium heat until the mixture turns into a custard and covers the back of a wooden spoon.
4. Put it through a fine-mesh strainer immediately, then put it in the fridge until it's completely cool. Then, freeze using an ice cream maker according to the directions that came with it.

22. PASSION FRUIT ICE CREAM

Prep Time: 15 Minutes | Cook Time: 5 Minutes | Total Time: 20 Minutes | Serving: 12

Ingredients

- 120 gr Passion Fruit Pulp
- 180 ml Heavy Cream
- 6 Egg Yolks
- 180 ml Whole Milk
- 80 gr Caster Sugar
- 1 1/2 tsp Vanilla Paste

Instructions

1. Put the milk, cream, and passion fruit pulp in a medium-sized saucepan along with the vanilla. Put it on low heat on the stove and whisk it together. Then, turn it up to high and let it simmer. Take it off the heat.
2. Put the egg yolks and sugar in a large bowl that can handle heat. Mix with a whisk until it's smooth.
3. Carefully pour the hot liquid over the eggs while you keep stirring them. Pour the whole thing back into the saucepan when it's smooth.
4. For 5 to 10 minutes, or until it gets thicker, cook it on low to medium-low heat. Putting the passion fruit through a fine mesh sieve will get rid of the seeds.
5. Put the food in a clean bowl, jar, or large, shallow pan. Put the custard in the fridge for at least three hours, or even better, overnight. Wrap it in plastic wrap that goes all the way to the top of the custard. You can put it in the freezer for 30 minutes before churning it if you want to.
6. Get the ice cream maker's bowl from the freezer and put it in the machine. Add the cool ice cream custard to the bowl, then turn it on. It should be whipped for 15 to 20 minutes or until it's like thick whipped cream.
7. Put the passion fruit ice cream in a clean container in the freezer. Freeze it for at least three hours before serving.

23. TIRAMISU ICE CREAM

Prep Time: 20 Minutes | Cook Time: 20 Minutes | Total Time: 40 Minutes | Serving: 6

Ingredients

- 1 cup of heavy cream
- 1 tsp instant espresso powder
- 1/2 cup of sugar
- 1/4 cup of espresso coffee
- 1 tsp vanilla
- 1 cup of whole milk
- 3 egg yolks
- 1 cup of Mascarpone
- 1/2 tsp Kahlua

Instructions

1. Turn the heat down to medium-low and add the milk and cream to the pan. Warm the milk up and stir it around.
2. Mix the egg yolks and sugar in a large bowl with a whisk until the mixture is pale and foamy. Mix in the mascarpone cheese until it's all mixed in.

3. Mix the egg yolks and mascarpone with a whisk of 1/2 cup of hot milk. Put the hot milk into the mixture and mix it all. Stir the custard for 5 to 8 minutes over medium warm until it gets thick enough to cover the back of a spoon.
4. Move the mixture to a bowl and let it cool down. You can put it in the fridge overnight or use an ice bath to speed up the process.
5. Set your ice cream machine to "mix, " then add the coffee powder, espresso, and liqueur.
6. Follow the steps with your ice cream maker to freeze it until it looks like soft-serve ice cream. Cover and freeze until firm. Move to a 9-by-13-inch pan that has been lined with parchment paper.
7. Serve and enjoy!

24. CHOCOLATE AND CHILLI ICE CREAM

Prep Time: 10 Minutes | Cook Time: 45 Minutes

Total Time: 55 Minutes | Serving: 4

Ingredients

- 6 tsp sugar
- 1 tbsp whiskey
- 3 egg yolks
- Crushed roasted hazel nuts
- 375ml full fat milk
- 1 tsp red chilli powder
- 375ml double cream
- 150g sweetened dark chocolate

Instructions

1. Put the cream, milk, and three tsp of sugar in a medium-sized saucepan.
2. Over medium heat, bring to a simmer. Then, turn down the heat a bit.
3. While that is going on, whisk the yolks until they are smooth and creamy. Then add the last three tsp of sugar and mix it in some more.
4. Add the egg yolks to the pan. If you let this mix bubble, the egg yolks will separate. It must only be cooked slowly until thick enough to cover a spoon.
5. Cut the chocolate into little chunks and add them to the pot.
6. Put the chocolate and stir it into the cream until it melts. Make sure the cream stays cool.
7. Stir the whisky and chili powder together after adding them. Make sure it's seasoned. 2 tsp of chili powder was used.
8. Let it cool down for a while.
9. Use this to fill up your ice cream machine, then turn it on. It will take about 30 minutes for the Buffalo Ice Cream Maker to make your ice cream.
10. Add the marshmallows or hazelnuts right at the end, about a minute before the ice cream is done.

25. GREEK YOGURT ICE CREAM

Prep Time: 10 Minutes | Cook Time: 00 Minutes

Total Time: 10 Minutes | Serving: 6

Ingredients

- 1 lemon
- 150 g confectioners
- 1 sprig lavender
- 150 g heavy cream
- honey
- 1 piece honey comb
- 450 g strained Greek yogurt

Instructions

1. Mix the yogurt, cream, and zest in the ice cream maker's container. Then, follow the manufacturer's instructions for how to use the machine.
2. Do not use an ice cream maker. Instead, mix everything by hand and put it in a metal container. Over the day, you will mix it by hand six times, or about every half hour.
3. Place a scoop of ice cream on a honeycomb slice, drizzle with honey, and top with a lavender sprig. Serve.

26. BERRY FROZEN YOGURT

Prep Time: 20 Minutes | Cook Time: 30 Minutes

Total Time: 50 Minutes | Serving: 6

Ingredients

- ½ tsp vanilla
- ¾ cup of fruit sugar
- ½ cup of heavy cream
- 1 cup of berries
- 1 tbsp corn syrup
- 3 cups of whole plain yogurt

Instructions

1. Whisk the yogurt, cream, vanilla, corn syrup, and refined sugar for about two minutes in a large bowl. Then, add the berries and mix them in.
2. Put the mix into the ice cream maker and churn it until thick. You can make it thicker if you want to. Serve right away. Put it in a container with a lid and freeze it for 3 to 6 hours, or overnight, until it gets firm like ice cream.
3. Take it out of the freezer and let it sit for 10 to 15 minutes before you serve it. Enjoy.
4. Before you use the ice cream maker, read the directions.

27. CHOCOLATE FROZEN YOGURT

Prep Time: 25 Minutes | Cook Time: 00 Minutes

Total Time: 25 Minutes | Serving: 8

Ingredients

- 1/2 tsp vanilla extract
- 2/3 cup of white granulated sugar
- 2 cups of full-fat vanilla bean yogurt
- 1/2 cup of heavy whipping cream
- 1/8 tsp fine sea salt
- 1/2 cup of Dutch-process cocoa powder

Instructions

1. Put the ingredients into a strong blender until the mixture is completely smooth. If you blended the mixture to warm it up, chill it down before putting it in an ice cream maker.
2. Once the ice cream maker is ready, follow the manufacturer's instructions for freezing the mixture. After making ice cream, eat the yogurt right away.
3. If you want, put the mixture in a container that won't let air in.

28. LEMON FROZEN YOGURT

Prep Time: 15 Minutes | Cook Time: 00 Minutes

Total Time: 15 Minutes | Serving: 4

Ingredients

- 1 cup of plain yogurt
- 1 cup of lemon curd

Instructions

1. Mix the yogurt and lemon curd together in a bowl to make it smooth. Leave to chill overnight.
2. Use your ice cream maker for 20 to 25 minutes in the morning to make the ice cream.

29. CINNAMON VANILLA BEAN GELATO

Prep Time: 15 Minutes | Cook Time: 20 Minutes

Total Time: 35 Minutes | Serving: 12

Ingredients

- 2 ¾ cups of whole milk
- ½ vanilla bean
- 1 ½ tsp vanilla
- 1 cinnamon stick
- 1 ¼ cups of heavy cream
- 1 1¼ cup of granulated sugar
- 2 tsp ground cinnamon
- 6 large egg yolks

Instructions

1. Mix 1 cup of sugar and whole milk in a heavy-bottomed medium saucepan. Mix well. Include the cinnamon stick, vanilla bean, and seeds. Stir occasionally over medium heat until an instant-read thermometer reads 170°F. Do not boil. Cover the bowl and leave it alone for 30 minutes to steep.

2. Take out the vanilla bean pod and cinnamon stick. Squeeze any vanilla seeds that are still in the pod into the milk. Put it back on medium heat and stir it occasionally until it reaches 170°F again. Mix the egg yolks and the last ¼ cup of sugar in a small bowl while the steeped mixture gets hot. Whisk until foamy and a little thicker.

3. Whisking continuously, slowly pour large spoonfuls of hot milk into the eggs to temper them. Whisk in more hot milk until half is incorporated into the eggs. Put the egg mixture back into the saucepan after tempering. Use a wooden spoon to stir it around until an instant-read thermometer reads 185°F. Take it off the heat and use a stick regular blender to blend it until it's smooth.

4. Put heavy cream in a large glass or stainless steel bowl over an ice bath. Put a fine mesh sieve over the cream. Pour hot custard through the sieve into cream and mix. Stir in pure vanilla extra and ground cinnamon. Keep stirring every 5 minutes until the mixture cools, about 30 minutes. Place in the fridge overnight with a tight lid. Process gelato in an ice cream maker per the manufacturer's instructions. Serve gelato after several hours of freezing in an airtight container. To preserve gelato, wrap it in plastic wrap and seal it in an airtight container.

30. PISTACHIO GELATO

Prep Time: 15 Minutes | Cook Time: 10 Minutes | Total Time: 25 Minutes | Serving: 6

Ingredients

For the Pistachio Paste:

- ➢ 1 cup of Shelled
- ➢ 1/2 cup of Granulated Sugar
- ➢ For the Pistachio Gelato:
- ➢ 1/2 tsp Lemon Zest

- ➢ 3 cups of Whole Milk
- ➢ Prepared Pistachio Paste
- ➢ 2 tbsp Cornstarch
- ➢ 1/2 cup of Granulated Sugar

Instructions

1. Start the water to boil. After that, turn off the heat and add the nuts.
2. Put the pistachios in water that is boiling for two to three minutes.
3. Then, drain the pistachios, rinse them under cold water, and use a paper towel to rub the skins off. Throw away the skins.
4. Put the pistachios in a food processor after blanching them and removing the skins. Break up the pistachios into tiny pieces in a food processor.
5. Clean the food processor's sides. Once you've added half a cup of sugar, keep grinding until it sticks together, like play dough but a little more grainy.
6. If you need to, scrape down the sides again and keep processing in the food processor until it turns into a smooth paste that sticks together.
7. Leave the pistachio mix alone.

31. HAZELNUT GELATO

Prep Time: 10 Minutes | Cook Time: 15 Minutes | Total Time: 25 Minutes | Serving: 8

Ingredients

- ➢ ⅓ cup of white sugar
- ➢ ½ cup of chocolate hazelnut spread
- ➢ ½ tsp vanilla extract
- ➢ 4 egg yolks

- ➢ ⅓ cup of white sugar
- ➢ 2 tbsp instant espresso powder
- ➢ 2 cups of whole milk
- ➢ 1 cup of heavy whipping cream

Instructions

1. Over medium heat, put milk, cream, and 1/3 cup of sugar in a saucepan. Cook and stir for 3-5 minutes or until the sugar is dissolved.
2. Egg yolks and 1/3 cup of sugar should be mixed in a bowl for about 4 minutes or until the colour turns light yellow. Put half of the milk mixture into the egg mixture & stir until the mixture is smooth. Then put the egg mixture to the rest of the milk mixture in the saucepan & stir it all the time. Keep stirring the mixture for 8 to 10 minutes or until it gets thick enough to coat the back of a metal spoon. Then, take it off the heat.

3. Add espresso powder, vanilla extract, and chocolate hazelnut spread to the milk mixture and stir until everything is well mixed. put the mixture through a mesh strainer into a bowl. For about three hours, or until cold, put the mixture in the fridge.
4. Add the milk mixture to an ice cream maker and freeze it according to the machine's directions.

32. STRACCIATELLA GELATO

Prep Time: 15 Minutes | Cook Time: 00 Minutes

Total Time: 15 Minutes | Serving: 8

Ingredients

- ➢ 4 egg yolks
- ➢ 1 vanilla bean
- ➢ 4 ounces bittersweet chocolate
- ➢ 1 cup of heavy cream
- ➢ 2 cups of whole milk
- ➢ 3/4 cup of sugar

Instructions

1. Put the vanilla bean in a medium-sized saucepan and heat it over medium-low. Then, stir the milk and sugar together. Warm it up until bubbles start to form around the edges. Take the pan off the heat and let it sit for 15 minutes.
2. Mix the egg yolks in a medium-sized bowl. Mix the warm milk and butter into the egg yolks slowly with a whisk. Then, return the mixture to the saucepan. Over medium-low heat, stir the custard constantly with a wooden spoon for 8-10 minutes or until it thickens and coats the back of the spoon. Remove from heat.
3. Put a mesh strainer on top of the cream in a large bowl. Take the vanilla bean from the custard and pour it through the sieve. Then, mix the custard into the cream. Cover and put in the fridge until it's cold.
4. Take custard out of the fridge and follow the manufacturer's instructions for making ice cream in an ice cream maker. Melt the chocolate in the microwave or a saute pan over low heat while making the ice cream. While the gelato is still being churned, slowly pour a skinny stream of the chocolate into it.

33. RASPBERRY SWIRL FROZEN YOGURT

Prep Time: 30 Minutes | Cook Time: 5 Minutes

Total Time: 35 Minutes | Serving: 8

Ingredients

For the Frozen Yogurt:

- 32 ounce whole yogurt
- 3 tbsp light-colored raw honey
- 1 tbsp organic vanilla extract
- ¼ tsp mineral-rich salt
- ½ tsp organic almond extract
- 1 tbsp arrowroot powder

For the Raspberry Swirl:

- 6 ounce fresh or frozen organic raspberries
- 3 tbsp light-colored raw honey

Instructions

1. Gather everything you need to make frozen yogurt and put it in a blender. Few pulses are enough to mix. Set aside.
2. Get the ice cream maker ready to go. To make ice cream, start the machine and pour the frozen yogurt mixture into it. Follow the directions on the package for churning.
3. Make the raspberry coulis while the frozen yoghurt is moving around. Heat the sweetener of your choice in a small saucepan and add the raspberries. Stir the raspberries around a few times a minute for about 5 minutes or until they break into a liquid puree. With a fine mesh strainer, pour the coulis into a mixing bowl. Then, put the raspberry coulis in the fridge to cool down.
4. To be done, the frozen yogurt should have a "soft serve" texture. Take the blender away from the frozen yogurt. With a wooden spoon, add ⅓ of the frozen yogurt to a container that can go in the freezer. Then, drizzle ⅓ of the cooled raspberry coulis over the ice cream. Do this again by adding another ⅓ of frozen yogurt to the first, then drizzle ⅓ of the raspberry coulis over the frozen yogurt. Finally, do this one last time by adding the last ⅓ of ice cream on top of the first, and then drizzle the rest of the raspberry coulis over the top. Put the dish in the freezer for about 15 minutes with the lid on, then serve immediately. A bit thicker than "soft serve" is the best way to serve this frozen yogurt. If it's been frozen for more than 15 minutes, take it out of the freezer and let it sit on the counter for at least 30 minutes before serving. Once it's fully frozen, it won't be as soft.

34. HONEY VANILLA FROZEN YOGURT

Prep Time: 5 Minutes | Cook Time: 00 Minutes

Total Time: 5 Minutes | Serving: 8

Ingredients
- 2/3 cup of heavy cream
- 1 Tbsp vanilla extract
- 2 1/3 cup of whole milk yogurt
- pinch salt
- 2/3 cup of honey

Instructions
1. Beat the yogurt, honey, salt, and vanilla in a bowl with a whisk until smooth.
2. Add the cream and mix it in with a whisk. Try to cool the mixture down if you can.
3. Follow the manufacturer's instructions when you churn your chilled mixture into an ice cream machine.
4. Spread the ice cream in a container that can go in the freezer. Freeze it for a few hours so that it gets firm before you serve it.

35. MINT CHIP FROZEN YOGURT

Prep Time: 30 Minutes | Cook Time: 00 Minutes

Total Time: 30 Minutes | Serving: 8

Ingredients
- 3 cups of whole-fat plain yogurt
- 1 1/2 cups of low-fat milk
- green food coloring
- 1 tsp peppermint extract
- 3/4 cup of sugar
- 3/4 cup of mini chocolate chips

Instructions
1. Your ice cream maker bowl should be frozen 24 hours before you want to make the frozen yogurt. A whisk should mix milk and sugar in a large bowl until all the sugar is gone. Use a whisk to combine the yogurt. Add half a tsp of peppermint extract and mix it. Then taste it and add another 1/2 tsp if you think it needs it.
2. Put the yogurt mixture into the bowl and follow the maker's instructions for freezing. Cover the frozen yogurt with a lid and freeze it for at least three hours. After that, put the chocolate chips and mix them in.

36. PEACH GELATO

Prep Time: 40 Minutes | Cook Time: 00 Minutes

Total Time: 40 Minutes | Serving: 12

Ingredients

- 1 cup of whole milk
- ½ cup of simple syrup
- ⅔ cup of sugar
- 2 cups of peaches
- 1 cup of heavy cream
- 1-2 tsp lemon juice

Instructions

1. Cut the peaches into small pieces. Put it in a big bowl or beaker. Add lemon juice and toss.
2. Put the rest of the ingredients into the beaker. Use a blender to completely puree the peaches and break up the sugar in the mixture.
3. Use the gelato setting on an ice cream maker and follow the manufacturer's instructions to chill.
4. Put the gelato that has been chilled in a tub or one-pint container. Put it in the fridge for at least an hour or overnight before you serve it.

37. YOGURT ICE CREAM

Prep Time: 5 Minutes | Cook Time: 25 Minutes

Total Time: 30 Minutes | Serving: 10

Ingredients

- 3 cups of non fat Greek yogurt
- ⅔ cup of white sugar
- 1 tsp vanilla extract

Instructions

1. Combine all the ingredients and mix them well until the sugar is gone.
2. For one hour, cover and put in the fridge.
3. Follow the steps on the ice cream maker to freeze the mixture.
4. Yugurt ice cream should be kept in a plastic container with plastic wrap on top of it.
5. It works best after being frozen for at least two hours.

SORBET & SHERBET

38. MANGO SORBET

Prep Time: 15 Minutes | Cook Time: 00 Minutes

Total Time: 15 Minutes | Serving: 12

Ingredients
- 4 mangos
- 3 tbsp fresh lime juice
- 1 cup of simple syrup

Instructions
1. Put mango cubes into a food processor and blend them until smooth. Put the lime juice and simple syrup and blend until the mixture is smooth.
2. Putting it in an ice cream machine. Freeze very well.

39. RASPBERRY LEMONADE SORBET

Prep Time: 15 Minutes | Cook Time: 5 Minutes

Total Time: 20 Minutes | Serving: 5

Ingredients
- 2 tbsp vodka
- ⅓ cup of lemon juice
- ¾ cup of granulated sugar
- 1.5 pounds frozen raspberries
- 1 cup of water

Instructions
1. Put your frozen raspberries into a blender or food processor with much power. Leave the raspberries alone to thaw at room temperature.
2. Put water and sugar in a medium-sized saucepan. Put it on high heat and stir or whisk it occasionally until the sugar is gone.
3. Put the simple syrup aside. Put the fresh lemon juice and zest and whisk them in. Let the mixture cool.
4. Put the simple syrup that has been cooled into the blender. Blend until the mixture is smooth.
5. Churn sorbet by following the directions on your ice cream maker.
6. Place a piece of parchment paper on top of the sorbet in your ice cream container. Freeze for 6 to 8 hours or even overnight. After letting it sit at room temperature for a while, serve it. Scoop it up and enjoy!

40. STRAWBERRY-BASIL SORBET

Prep Time: 20 Minutes | Cook Time: 00 Minutes

Total Time: 20 Minutes | Serving: 4

Ingredients

- 3/4 cup of granulated sugar
- 1 tsp freshly squeezed lemon juice
- 1/4 cup of freshly chopped basil
- 1 pound. fresh strawberries rinsed

Instructions

1. Put the strawberries and sugar in a medium-sized bowl and toss them around. Make sure to mix the strawberries well so that they are all covered. Put the lid on top and stir it around a few times during the hour.
2. To smooth the sauce, blend or process the strawberries, basil, and lemon juice in a blend.
3. After letting the mixture cool down all the way, follow the directions that came with your ice cream maker to freeze it.

41. BLUEBERRY SORBET

Prep Time: 20 Minutes | Cook Time: 00 Minutes

Total Time: 20 Minutes | Serving: 8

Ingredients

- 1/4 cup of sugar
- 1 tbsp lemon juice
- 5 cups of fresh or frozen blueberries
- Pinch salt
- 1/4 cup of honey
- Fresh blueberries
- 1 tsp lemon zest

Instructions

1. Sugar, lemon zest, honey, lemon juice, and salt should all be put in a large bowl. Use a spoon to coat the blueberries with the sugar. I used a potato masher to mash it.
2. To smooth the blueberry sauce, put the mashed blueberries in a blender and blend for a few minutes.
3. Set up a sieve over a large bowl. Press the mixture through the sieve one batch at a time using a rubber spatula. This will catch the bigger, tougher pieces of blueberry and lemon peel.
4. Put the mix in the fridge for at least an hour. Then, do what your ice cream maker says and follow the steps.
5. You can eat it right away or freeze it for at least a few hours to help it set up before you eat it. The sorbet will get harder the longer it stays in the freezer, so eat it as soon as possible after making it.
6. Add some fresh blueberries and a mint sprig to the serving bowl.

42. LEMON SORBET

Prep Time: 15 Minutes | Cook Time: 00 Minutes

Total Time: 15 Minutes | Serving: 6

Ingredients

- ➢ 6 strips of lemon zest
- ➢ ½ cup of carbonated mineral water
- ➢ ½ cup of sugar
- ➢ 1 cup of water
- ➢ ½ cup of lemon juice
- ➢ 1 lemon's peel

Instructions

1. Put sugar, diced lemon peel, and 1 cup of water in a saucepan. Stir them together and bring to a boil. Then, slow the heat to medium and let it simmer for 5 minutes. Take it off the heat and let it cool down.
2. Mix lemon peel syrup, lemon juice, and mineral water in a pitcher or bowl. Put it in an ice cream maker and freeze it the way the machine says to. Serve each one with a twist of lemon peel on top.
3. There is a way to freeze ice cream if you still need an ice cream maker. Put it in the freezer for one and a half hours. Take it out and use a whisk to mix it. While it's frozen, stir it about once an hour for four hours. The mixture will be lighter because more air will be mixed in the more you stir it.

43. PINEAPPLE COCONUT SORBET

Prep Time: 15 Minutes | Cook Time: 00 Minutes

Total Time: 15 Minutes | Serving: 8

Ingredients

- ➢ 1 tsp grated ginger root
- ➢ 3/4 cup of sugar
- ➢ Pinch salt
- ➢ 1 tbsp chopped lemongrass
- ➢ 1 1/4 cup of pineapple juice
- ➢ 1 tbsp lime zest
- ➢ 1 tbsp lime juice
- ➢ 1 can coconut milk
- ➢ 1/4 cup of agave syrup

Instructions

1. Put sugar, agave syrup, lime juice, lemongrass, lime zest, ginger root, and salt in a small saucepan. Stir them together. Bring to a simmer and stir it occasionally until the sugar is gone. Put the coconut milk and mix it in.
2. Put the saucepan in a bowl of ice water or the fridge until cold to chill the sorbet base. Put into an ice cream maker & follow the manufacturer's instructions for how to make ice cream. Put the sorbet in a container that can be sealed and freeze it until it gets firm. You can also eat it while it's still soft and creamy.

44. WATERMELON SORBET

Prep Time: 10 Minutes | Cook Time: 5 Minutes

Total Time: 15 Minutes | Serving: 8

Ingredients

- ¼ cup of lemon juice
- 3 cups of cubed seeded watermelon
- ½ cup of water
- 1 cup of white sugar

Instructions

1. Take the pan off high heat and mix the sugar, water, and lemon juice. Stir the food and cook for about five minutes or until the sugar is gone. Take it off the heat and let it cool in the fridge for 30 minutes.
2. The watermelon should be blended with a blender until it is smooth. Add the sugar and watermelon puree and mix them. Put the watermelon mix into an ice cream maker and freeze it according to the maker's instructions until it's the consistency you want.

45. BLACKBERRY SHERBET

Prep Time: 15 Minutes | Cook Time: 00 Minutes

Total Time: 15 Minutes | Serving: 16

Ingredients

- 4 cups of fresh or frozen blackberries
- 4 cups of buttermilk
- 2 tsp vanilla
- 2 cups of sugar

Instructions

1. The ice cream maker's container should be chilled in the fridge while the sherbet mixture is made.
2. If you need to, scrape down the sides of the blender or food processor as you go to make the blackberries smooth. To get the seeds out of the blackberry puree, run it through a strainer.
3. Combine the vanilla, buttermilk, and sugar in a bowl. Mix the ingredients by stirring them together. Use the ice cream freezer's churn and freeze settings as the machine's maker directs.

46. KIWI SORBET

Prep Time: 15 Minutes | Cook Time: 00 Minutes

Total Time: 15 Minutes | Serving: 2

Ingredients

- 2 tbsp Lemon Juice
- 6-7 Kiwi
- 1 cup of water
- 1/2 cup of sugar

Instructions

1. Start by cutting the brown fur into small pieces after peeling it off.
2. Then, blend or process all the kiwis until you get about 2 cups of puree.
3. To make a simple syrup, boil 1 cup of water and half cup of sugar in a small saucepan. Take it off the heat and let it cool down. I put the syrup into a glass measuring cup in an ice bath to cool down faster.
4. Put kiwi puree, syrup, and two tbsp of lemon juice into the ice cream maker. Then, do what the maker says.

47. BLOOD ORANGE SORBET

Prep Time: 10 Minutes | Cook Time: 5 Minutes

Total Time: 15 Minutes | Serving: 3

Ingredients

- 2 tbsp champagne
- 1 tbsp lemon juice
- 2 cups of-blood orange juice
- 1/2 cup of sugar
- 1 cup of water
- Zest from one blood orange

Instructions

1. Take the zest off of one orange and set it aside. Two cups of blood orange juice should come out of them.
2. Heat the water, lemon zest, lemon juice, and 1/2 cup of sugar in a small size saucepan over medium heat. Stir the sugar in often until it dissolves. It shouldn't be too hot, just warm enough to melt the sugar.
3. A small amount of white wine, champagne, or orange liqueur should be added along with the blood orange juice. This is not required.
4. Put it in the fridge for a long time, and then use an ice cream or sorbet maker to churn it until it reaches the consistency you want.
5. Best eaten right away!

48. APRICOT SHERBET

Prep Time: 10 Minutes | Cook Time: 00 Minutes

Total Time: 10 Minutes | Serving: 6

Ingredients

- 2 cups of water
- 1/8 tsp xanthan gum
- 1/8 tsp almond extract
- 3/4 cup of dried apricots
- 1/2 cup of allulose
- 1 tbsp lemon juice
- 1 tsp apricot extract

Instructions

1. In the bowl of a strong blender, mix the apricots and allulose. Put in the boiling water and let it sit for 30 minutes to get soft. Mix in the rest of the ingredients until the mix is smooth.
2. Put it into an ice cream maker and churn it according to the machine's directions. You could also put it in a container that can go in the freezer and freeze it for three hours, stirring now and then to break up any crystals.
3. Put in a container that can go in the freezer and freeze until firm.

49. GRAPEFRUIT SORBET

Prep Time: 20 Minutes | Cook Time: 20 Minutes

Total Time: 40 Minutes | Serving: 6

Ingredients

- 1 1/2 cup of fresh grapefruit juice
- 1 tbsp granulated sugar
- 1 1/4 cups of water
- 1 tbsp grapefruit zest

Instructions

1. In a saucepan over medium to high heat, mix water and sugar. Heat it and stir it around until there is no more sugar.
2. Take it off the heat, add the zest, and let it cool down. After it's cool, add the grapefruit juice, stir, cover, and put it in the fridge for two hours or until it's freezing.
3. Following the directions that came with your ice cream maker, churn it once it's frozen.
4. You can serve it immediately or put it in the freezer until you're ready.

50. LIME SHERBET

Prep Time: 30 Minutes | Cook Time: 00 Minutes

Total Time: 30 Minutes | Serving: 6

Ingredients

- 3 cups of whole milk
- ¾ cup of sugar
- 2 Tbsp lime zest
- 1 cup of fresh squeezed lime juice

Instructions

1. Peel the limes. Use a knife to cut the zest into smaller pieces if you want.
2. Get the lime juice.
3. Mix in the sugar and stir until it's gone.
4. Put it in a big bowl and add milk and orange zest. The lime juice will make the milk look a little curdled and thicken it. It's okay!
5. Follow the manufacturer's instructions for churning and pour into your ice cream maker. Churn for 20 to 30 minutes or until frozen.
6. Put the sherbet in a container that can go in the freezer and freeze it for at least two hours to make it hard.

51. PEPPERMINT MOCHA ICE CREAM

Prep Time: 10 Minutes | Cook Time: 00 Minutes

Total Time: 10 Minutes | Serving: 6

Ingredients

- 1½ cups of heavy cream
- ⅛ tsp kosher salt
- ⅔ cup of sugar
- ¼ tsp peppermint extract
- ½ tsp vanilla extract
- 1½ cup of whole milk
- 2 tsp cocoa powder

Instructions

1. Mix the cream, milk, sugar, cocoa powder, and salt in a small saucepan. Warm the mix over medium-low heat until the sugar and cocoa are completely mixed in. Take the pot off the heat and immediately add the vanilla and peppermint extracts. Bring it all together, and then let it cool down.
2. When you are ready to make ice cream, whisk the mixture and pour it into the machine. Follow the directions on the package for churning.
3. When the ice cream is done, put it in a container that won't let air in and freeze it until you're ready to serve it. You can sprinkle chocolate shavings on top if you want to.

52. GINGERBREAD ICE CREAM

Prep Time: 35 Minutes | Cook Time: 00 Minutes

Total Time: 35 Minutes | Serving: 6

Ingredients
- 1 cup of low-fat milk
- 2/3 cup of sugar
- 1/4 tsp freshly grated nutmeg
- 1 tsp cinnamon
- 2 tsp ground ginger
- 2 Tbsp molasses
- 1 cup of heavy cream
- 1/2 tsp allspice
- 1/4 tsp ground cloves

Instructions
1. In a large bowl, mix everything using a whisk. Make sure you stir for a long time to mix the sugar and molasses fully.
2. To make ice cream, use an ice cream maker and do what it says on the box. It takes me twenty-five minutes to make ice cream.
3. Layer the ice cream in a container, wrap it in plastic wrap, and freeze it. This will toughen it up. Do this four to six hours ahead of time for best results, or leave it overnight.

53. PUMPKIN PIE ICE CREAM

Prep Time: 20 Minutes | Cook Time: 30 Minutes

Total Time: 50 Minutes | Serving: 8

Ingredients
- 1 cup of heavy whipping cream
- 1 tsp vanilla extract
- 1 1/2 cups of half and half
- 1/2 cup of packed brown sugar
- 1/4 tsp salt
- 1 1/2 cups of whole milk
- 1 cup of pumpkin pie filling
- 1/2 cup of granulated sugar
- 6 graham crackers

Instructions
1. Mix the sugars, salt, and vanilla into the pumpkin pie filling.
2. Mix in the half-and-half, milk, and whipped cream. Mix everything.
3. Put it in the ice cream maker and do what it says.
4. When the ice cream is almost done, add broken cookies or crackers and process for a few more minutes to mix the cookies into the ice cream.
5. To set up, put the ice cream in an insulation container and in the freezer.

54. GINGER MAPLE MISO ICE CREAM

Prep Time: 5 Minutes | Cook Time: 5 Minutes

Total Time: 10 Minutes | Serving: 8

Ingredients

- 2 cans full fat coconut milk
- ¾ cup of crystallized ginger
- ⅓ cup of maple syrup
- 1 tbsp pure vanilla
- 2 tbsp tapioca starch
- 1-2 tbsp miso paste

Instructions

1. Start with 1 tbsp of miso and add more if you like it more salty.
2. Add 2 tbsp of tapioca starch to a small bowl and mix them using a whisk. Save for later.
3. Then, put the rest of the coconut milk in the pan and set it on medium-low heat. Stirring and lowering the heat to a simmer will take five minutes.
4. Mix the tapioca starch with maple syrup and miso. Add these to the saucepan. Stir the mixture even as it gets thicker. Let it cool down after taking it off the heat.
5. Put the ice cream mix into the maker and follow the manufacturer's instructions.
6. Cut up the crystallized ginger into small pieces while making the ice cream.
7. Add ½ cup of crystallized ginger while the machine is still running to make ice cream.
8. Keep going for another few minutes until the ginger is fully mixed in. Put the mixture in a container that can go in the freezer, top with the rest of the ginger crystals, and freeze.

55. PISTACHIO ICE CREAM

Prep Time: 15 Minutes | Cook Time: 25 Minutes

Total Time: 40 Minutes | Serving: 10

Ingredients

- 2 cups of whipping cream
- 1 tsp vanilla
- ¾ cup of chopped pistachios
- 1 cup of shelled pistachios
- ¾ cup of sugar
- 1 cup of milk

Instructions

1. Put 1 cup of pistachios and the sugar in a food processor. Mix until the mixture is very fine. You may need to stir the nuts to ensure they are all gone.
2. Milk and ground pistachios should be put in a medium-sized saucepan.
3. Stir the mixture around a lot over medium-low heat until it boils.
4. Take it off the heat and let it cool down.
5. Putting it in the fridge for about two hours will help it cool completely.
6. Add the vanilla and whipped cream and mix well.
7. Put the mix into the ice cream maker.
8. Mix for about 20 to 25 minutes or as directed by the manufacturer.

9. Add chopped pistachios to the ice cream that is being made.
10. Blend for five more minutes. You'll enjoy this tasty ice cream!

56. RUM RAISIN ICE CREAM

Prep Time: 10 Minutes | Cook Time: 5 Minutes

Total Time: 15 Minutes | Serving: 12

Ingredients

- 1 cup of raisins
- 1 tbsp pure vanilla extract
- 2 cups of whipping cream
- 2 cups of whole milk
- 1 cup of sugar
- 6 egg yolks
- 4 ounces dark or amber rum

Instructions

1. In a container that won't let air in, soak the raisins in the rum overnight. To make sure the raisins are evenly soaked, I like to use a mason jar and shake it every so often.
2. Put the milk and cream together and heat them in the microwave or over medium-low heat on the stovetop until hot but not boiling.
3. Using a medium-sized saucepan, whisk the egg yolks and sugar together for three minutes or until the mixture is light and airy.
4. Blend the egg yolks slowly while adding a cup of hot milk. This keeps the egg yolks from cooking and scrambling. Mix in another cup by whisking it into the egg yolk mixture well. Finally, add the rest of the cream and scaled milk to ensure it's well mixed in.
5. Put the pan on medium-low heat and stir the mixture slowly and steadily for five minutes or until it gets thicker. You should now be able to dip the wooden spoon in the custard and use your finger to make a clear line on the back of the spoon. If you boil the mixture, it might separate.
6. Turn off the heat and put in the vanilla extract. Wait a few hours or overnight to let the custard cool completely. Let the raisins soak in the rum overnight while I put it in the fridge.
7. Mix the custard well and pour it into your ice cream maker once it is completely cold. Do this for twenty to thirty minutes or until the ice cream is as thick as possible.
8. Quickly move the ice cream to a cold metal or glass bowl and mix in the raisins that have been soaked in rum and any extra rum they haven't soaked up.
9. Put in a container that won't let air in and freeze in the deep freezer or the coldest part of your fridge freezer. At least a few hours or, better yet, overnight before serving.
10. At least once every two hours, I fold the ice cream to ensure that the raisins don't all settle to the bottom of the container and are spread out evenly in the ice cream.

57. CARAMEL APPLE ICE CREAM

Prep Time: 30 Minutes | Cook Time: 15 Minutes

Total Time: 45 Minutes | Serving: 12

Ingredients

➢ 1 can of Sweetened Condensed Milk
➢ 2 cups of peeled cooking apples
➢ 1 cup of apple cider
➢ 1 ½ cups of half-and-half cream
➢ 2 tbsp butter
➢ ⅓ cup of Smuckers Caramel Flavored Topping
➢ ¾ tsp apple pie spice

Instructions

1. Add the apple to melt the butter in a large skillet over medium-low heat. Cook the apple for about 10 minutes, stirring now and then, until it is soft. Add apple cider and apple pie spice, mix well, then cover and let it cook for 5 minutes.
2. If you put sweetened condensed milk and cream in a medium bowl, mix them using a whisk. Add the apple mix and stir. Add ice cubes and very cold water to a large bowl until it's about half full. Put the medium bowl with the ice cream mix inside the large bowl. It will take about 5 to 10 minutes of stirring until it is very cold.
3. Following the directions that came with your ice cream maker, freeze it. Utilize a pan that is 8 or 9 inches square to hold it. Soak the food in the freezer for three hours or until it is firm. After taking a scoop, put a lot of ice cream in the pan. Place the caramel topping on the ice cream and let it soak in. Repaint the pan with ice cream. Sock it up in the freezer until you're ready to serve.

58. RHUBARB ICE CREAM

Prep Time: 20 Minutes | Cook Time: 20 Minutes

Total Time: 40 Minutes | Serving: 10

Ingredients

Raspberries:

- 1/2 cup of sugar
- 2 cups of rhubarb
- 1 tbsp lemon juice

Ice Cream Base:

- 2 cups of heavy cream
- ¾ cup of milk
- ½-1 tsp cinnamon
- 1 tsp vanilla

Instructions

Rhubarb:

1. In a saucepan, stir the rhubarb, sugar, and lemon juice together.
2. While cooking, stir the rhubarb and sugar now and then.
3. Rhubarb should be cooked until it gets soft and starts to separate.
4. Put it in the fridge for three hours or until it's completely cold.

Ice Cream Base:

1. Mix the rhubarb and milk well.
2. Mix in the vanilla, cinnamon, and whipped cream.
3. Use an ice cream maker to make it.
4. Churn for about 20 minutes or as directed by the manufacturer.
5. Have fun with this summer treat!

59. SPICED CRANBERRY ICE CREAM

Prep Time: 15 Minutes | Cook Time: 5 Minutes

Total Time: 20 Minutes | Serving: 8

Ingredients

- 1/4 tsp ground allspice
- 3/4 cup of granulated sugar
- 1 1/2 cups of fresh cranberries
- 2 tbsp bourbon
- 2 cups of heavy cream
- ½ tsp orange extract
- 1 cup of water

Instructions

1. Put the orange extract, water, sugar, and berries in a small saucepan and set it over medium-high heat. Bring to a boil, then turn off the heat and cover. Boil for one minute. Allow to sit for 30 minutes.
2. Place the fine disk of a food mill over a medium-sized bowl. But what's in the saucepan into the food mill, and then turn the crank to push the cranberries through. Make sure to get any puree stuck to the disk's bottom and put it in the bowl. Throw away skins.
3. Combine heavy cream, bourbon, and allspice. Mix the ingredients well. Leave the bowl covered for at least four hours to cool down.
4. Then, put it in the bowl of an ice cream maker and let it chill as the maker's instructions say.

60. CINNAMON TOAST CRUNCH ICE CREAM

Prep Time: 30 Minutes | Cook Time: 00 Minutes

Total Time: 30 Minutes | Serving: 8

Ingredients

- 1½ cups of half & half
- ¼ tsp salt
- 1/4 cup of brown sugar
- 1 cup of sugar
- 3 cups of Cinnamon Toast Crunch cereal
- 1½ Tbsp pure vanilla
- 1½ cups of whole milk
- extra cereal for garnish
- 2 cups of whipping cream
- 1 tsp cinnamon

Instructions

1. After adding 2 cups of cereal to 1.5 cups of whole milk, let it sit for 30 to 45 minutes.
2. Take the cereal out of the milk and throw away the wet cereal.
3. Add cereal, sugar, cinnamon, salt, half-and-half, vanilla, and whipped cream to the milk. After that, put the mix into an ice cream maker.
4. Follow the directions given by the manufacturer.

5. For the last cup of cereal, sprinkle brown sugar on it while you make the ice cream. Add the cereal to a pan with medium-low heat and melt the brown sugar. Combine the cereal with melted sugar and mix it well.
6. Put it on a plate and let it cool down. Cut up.
7. Once the ice cream is smooth, add the sugared cereal and mix it in. Then, freeze it in a container until it gets hard.
8. If you want, you can add more cereal as a garnish when you serve it.

61. CANDY CANE ICE CREAM

Prep Time: 10 Minutes | Cook Time: 00 Minutes

Total Time: 10 Minutes | Serving: 8

Ingredients

- ½ tsp peppermint extract
- ¾ cup of very finely crushed candy canes
- ⅛ tsp kosher salt
- 2 tsp vanilla extract
- 1½ cups of heavy cream
- ½ cup of sugar
- 1½ cups of milk

Add-Ins:

- 1 cup of peppermint bark
- ⅓ cup of COLD chocolate sauce
- ¼ cup of additional crushed candy canes

Instructions

1. Mix the candy and milk in a blender or food processor by pulsing them a few times.
2. The sugar, vanilla, peppermint extract, and salt should all be mixed with a whisk. Mix the peppermint candy with the milk. Put the mixture into your ice cream maker and follow the directions on the box.
3. Move a third of the churned ice cream to a freezer container that won't let air in. If you want, you can drizzle chocolate sauce over the top and sprinkle with candy cane pieces. Add chopped peppermint bark on top. Do the layers twice more.
4. For soft serve ice cream, serve right away or freeze until firm.

62. CHOCOLATE ICE CREAM WITH MARSHMALLOWS

Prep Time: 10 Minutes | Cook Time: 5 Minutes

Total Time: 15 Minutes | Serving: 8

Ingredients

- ➢ 1 tsp cornstarch
- ➢ 8 ounces of mini marshmallows store-bought
- ➢ 1 1/4 cups of heavy cream
- ➢ 1/8 tsp salt
- ➢ 2 cups of whole milk
- ➢ 1/2 cup of granulated sugar
- ➢ 2 Tbsp light corn syrup
- ➢ 1/2 cup of sifted hot chocolate mix
- ➢ 3 ounces cream cheese

Instructions

1. Put the cornstarch and 2 tbsp of milk in a small bowl and mix them with a whisk.
2. Mix the salt and cream cheese in a bowl that can handle heat until smooth.
3. Add the heavy cream, sugar, corn syrup, and milk to a medium-sized saucepan. Use a whisk to mix the ingredients. Over medium-high heat, bring to a boil. Boil for 4 minutes, stirring now and then. Using a whisk, add the cornstarch mix. Bring it back to a boil and stir it all the time with a heat-safe spatula for about one minute or until it gets a little thicker.
4. Before adding the hot milk, mix it with the cream cheese until it's smooth. Put the dish in the fridge with the lid on for several hours or overnight to thoroughly chill.
5. Get the marshmallows ready at the same time. Cut the marshmallows you make yourself into small pieces. Wrap a big cookie sheet in foil and grease it a little. Cover the pan with marshmallows all over. The bread can be toasted with a kitchen torch or under the broiler. It should be frozen for two hours.
6. Following the steps that came with your ice cream maker will help it freeze once it's cold enough. If you want to freeze the ice cream, add the marshmallows to it after you've churned it. Make sure to freeze it.

63. COCONUT MILK ICE CREAM

Prep Time: 10 Minutes | Cook Time: 00 Minutes

Total Time: 10 Minutes | Serving: 10

Ingredients

- 2 tsp powdered sunflower lecithin
- 1 can full-fat coconut milk
- 3 large pitted Medjool dates
- 1 Tbsp pure vanilla extract
- 1 can unsweetened coconut cream
- ⅛ tsp sea salt
- ⅓ cup of sugar

Instructions

1. For ice cream makers with removable canisters, take the food out of the freezer at least 24 hours before making the ice cream.
2. Before opening, shake the coconut milk cans. Add the sugar, dates, vanilla, and salt to a high-speed blender. Also, add the coconut milk or cream. The dates should be completely mixed in with the motor running at full speed for about one minute. Blend again after adding the lecithin if you're using it.
3. Following the ice cream machine's instructions, churn the coconut ice cream mix. For scoopable ice cream, move it to a freezer-safe or individual-serving container, cover it, and freeze it for about 4 hours. Once it reaches soft-serve consistency, you can eat it right away. Place on a flat surface and let it soften for a few minutes.

64. VEGAN DARK CHOCOLATE ALMOND ICE CREAM

Prep Time: 15 Minutes | Cook Time: 00 Minutes

Total Time: 15 Minutes | Serving: 6

Ingredients

- 1/2 tsp vanilla extract
- 1/4 cup of dark chocolate covered almonds
- 1 tsp unsulphured molasses
- 1/4 cup of cocoa powder
- 2 tbsp pure maple syrup
- 1/8 tsp fine sea salt
- One 13.5 ounce can of full-fat canned coconut milk
- 90g dark cacao chocolate bar

Instructions

1. Put the chocolate powder, syrup, molasses, and coconut milk in a blender. Blend until the mixture is smooth.
2. In a double boiler or microwave bowl, melt your chocolate bar by breaking it up into small pieces for 30 seconds. This needs to be done 15 times to melt most of the chocolate.

More heat than necessary will burn the chocolate. Combine everything before it's smooth. It should be mixed with a blender. High-speed blending will make the mixture smooth.

3. Blend again after adding the sea salt and vanilla.

4. Put the mix into the machine that makes ice cream. Allow the machine to work its magic until it reaches the soft serve stage, and be careful not to stir it too much.

5. As it's churning, cut up the chocolate-covered nuts. You can add more or less, but this was enough for me. Once your ice cream has a soft serve consistency, put it in a container for ice cream. Spread the ice cream out and add the chopped chocolate almonds. Put a plastic wrap on top of the ice cream, then tighten the lid. Put it in the back of the freezer for two hours to get firm before you eat it. Eating homemade ice cream within a couple of days is best so ice crystals don't form.

65. MATCHA ICE CREAM

Prep Time: 30 Minutes | Cook Time: 00 Minutes

Total Time: 30 Minutes | Serving: 6

Ingredients

- ➤ 5 tbsp sugar
- ➤ 3 tbsp matcha powder
- ➤ 7 tbsp agave nectar
- ➤ ½ cup of chocolate chips
- ➤ 2 cans of coconut milk
- ➤ ⅛ tsp salt

Instructions

1. At least 24 hours should pass before you start making ice cream in the machine's bowl. Make sure the ice cream has the right consistency by doing this!

2. Blend the matcha powder, sugar, agave nectar, and salt until the mixture is completely smooth. Place the bowl in the fridge for at least an hour to cool down after pouring the mixture.

3. The ice cream maker should be turned on, and the container should be put in it. Then, slowly pour in the chilled matcha mixture. The mix of matcha and sugar will get thicker until it becomes a soft serve after running the ice cream maker. This takes about 10 to 15 minutes, but the time can vary a lot, so use your ice cream maker's instructions and look to see if it's done.

4. Using a spatula, quickly scoop all the soft ice cream into a storage container as soon as the ice cream maker is done. Then, fold the chocolate in gently. It will melt quickly because the ice cream is very soft, so cover it quickly and put it in the freezer as soon as you're done!

5. Put it in the freezer for at least 4 hours first, then eat it!

66. COCONUT AVOCADO ICE CREAM

Prep Time: 40 Minutes | Cook Time: 00 Minutes

Total Time: 40 Minutes | Serving: 6

Ingredients
- 1 1/2 tbsp fresh lemon juice
- 2 ripe medium avocados
- 1 can sweetened condensed milk
- 1/4 cup of sugar
- 1 can coconut milk

Instructions
1. Prepare avocados by cutting them in half. To smooth the flesh, put it in a food processor with sugar and lemon juice. Mix in the coconut milk and sweetened condensed milk by spinning the mixture.
2. In an ice cream maker, freeze the mixture as it says to. Put ice in a metal bowl.
3. Put ice cream into a bowl that is already cold. Freeze with the lid on for about two hours or until it's firm enough to scoop. Acquire real coconut milk for a mild taste. Get something that is made with coconut extract for a stronger coconut hit.
4. Do ahead of time: For up to two weeks, freeze airtight.

67. MANGO COCONUT SORBET ICE CREAM

Prep Time: 20 Minutes | Cook Time: 00 Minutes

Total Time: 20 Minutes | Serving: 3

Ingredients
- 1/2 cup of shredded coconut
- 1 large mango
- 1 can full-fat coconut milk
- 1/2 cup of water
- 2 tbsp lime juice
- 1/4 cup of cold water
- 1/2 cup of sugar

Instructions
1. Add sugar and half the water to a small pot or microwave bowl. After the sugar is dissolved, turn down the heat and let it cook slowly for 30 seconds.
2. Put the shredded coconut and mix it in. Then, wait about one minute until the coconut turns clear.
3. Thoroughly stir the sugar syrup into the coconut milk after shaking it.
4. Put in the fridge or an ice bath until it's cool.
5. Mix the mango chunks with 1/4 cup of water and lime juice.
6. Chill the mixture until it is very cold, then fold the mango.
7. Put it into the ice cream maker and let it run as the machine directs.
8. For firmer sorbet, freeze it for at least an hour in a container that can go in the freezer and has a lid that fits tightly on top. It can be served right away or for a long time after it's been frozen.

68. PEANUT BUTTER BANANA ICE CREAM

Prep Time: 10 Minutes | Cook Time: 00 Minutes

Total Time: 10 Minutes | Serving: 3

Ingredients
- 3 Tbsp all-natural peanut butter
- pinch of salt
- 1/2 tsp vanilla extract
- 3 frozen bananas

Instructions
1. To make them cook faster, cut the frozen bananas into coins. Then, put them in a big food processor bowl with an "S" blade. Also, add the vanilla, salt, and peanut butter.
2. Stop the food processor for smooth bananas and scrape the sides down as needed. Three to two minutes of processing will turn it into soft-serve consistency. But remember that adding a tbsp of water or almond milk could make your ice cream runnier.
3. Put the ice cream in a jar with a lid and freeze it for one or two hours. You should be able to scoop it up. Right away, serve soft serve. It will stay good for up to two weeks if you store banana ice cream in a container without air.

69. ALMOND JOY COCONUT ICE CREAM

Prep Time: 20 Minutes | Cook Time: 00 Minutes

Total Time: 20 Minutes | Serving: 4

Ingredients
- 2 cups of full-fat coconut milk
- 1/3 cup of shredded coconut
- 1/4 cup of maple syrup
- 1 tsp vanilla extract
- 1/4 cup of chocolate chips
- 1/3 cup of almonds sliced
- 3 organic or pastured egg yolks

Instructions
1. In a saucepan, mix the egg yolks, maple syrup, and coconut milk with a whisk.
2. Warm it up over medium-low heat and stir it often until it simmer.
3. Stir the mixture all the time for two minutes after it starts to simmer.
4. Take it off the heat and add the vanilla extract.
5. Mix everything well.
6. Put the mixture through a fine-mesh strainer set on top of a bowl.
7. Put the mixture in the fridge with the lid on for at least two hours to chill.
8. Pour into an ice cream maker after it has cooled down. Do the work for 10 minutes.
9. Put in the almonds, chocolate chips, and coconut.
10. After another 10 minutes of processing, the ice cream should be well-mixed and firm.
11. This ice cream will melt quickly, so don't leave it out for too long before eating it! Enjoy!

70. DAIRY-FREE MAPLE PECAN ICE CREAM

Prep Time: 10 Minutes | Cook Time: 00 Minutes

Total Time: 10 Minutes | Serving: 2

Ingredients

- 2 cups of pecans
- ½ cup of maple syrup

Instructions

1. Put the pecans in a bowl and add water to cover them. Soak the nuts for 8 to 10 hours at room temperature or in the fridge.
2. Save 1 cup of water to soak the pecans and drain them.
3. Put the pecans, the maple syrup, and the 1 cup of water you saved in a high-speed blender. Mix until smooth.
4. Pour it into your ice cream maker through a fine-mesh sieve and set it up according to the directions on the package.

71. BANANA COCONUT GINGER ICE CREAM

Prep Time: 15 Minutes | Cook Time: 00 Minutes

Total Time: 15 Minutes | Serving: 4

Ingredients

- 2 1/2 tbsp. desiccated coconut
- 3 bananas
- 1 tbsp. fresh ginger
- 1/2 tsp. alcohol-free vanilla extract
- 2 tbsp. grade A maple syrup

Instructions

1. Put everything into a food processor and blend it until it's pretty smooth and creamy.
2. If you want to mix everything well, stop blending, scrape the sides, and then begin blending again.
3. You can eat right away if you like soft serve. If you want ice cream, put the mixture in a container that can go in the freezer, cover it, and freeze it for two to four hours before serving.
4. When it's time to eat, use an ice cream scoop to put it in bowls. Enjoy yourself!

72. VEGAN SALTED CARAMEL ICE CREAM

Prep Time: 20 Minutes | Cook Time: 50 Minutes

Total Time: 1 Hour 10 Minutes | Serving: 8

Ingredients

Salted Caramel Ice Cream:

- 1 Pinch Sea Salt
- ½ cup of Coconut Sugar
- 14 ounces of Canned Coconut Cream
- ¼ cup of Golden Syrup
- 1 tsp Vanilla Extract
- 14 ounces of Canned Coconut Milk

Salted Caramel Sauce:

- ½ cup of Coconut Cream
- 6 Tbsp Vegan Butter
- 1 tsp Salt
- 1 cup of White Granulated Sugar
- 2 Tbsp Water
- ¼ cup of Maple Syrup

Instructions

Salted Caramel Ice Cream:

1. Put the ice cream maker's freezer bowl in the freezer the night before you want to make ice cream.
2. Set the pot on the stove and add the coconut cream, coconut milk, coconut sugar, and syrup.
3. Take the food off the heat, add the salt and vanilla extract, and blend it for 30 seconds with an immersion blender. This gets rid of any roughness in the texture.
4. Not having an immersion blender? You can use your blender jug instead. Be careful, though, because it will be very hot.
5. Put the ice cream mix in a lid jar in the fridge overnight.
6. Fill your ice cream maker with the mixture and churn it according to the maker's instructions when you're ready to make the ice cream the next day. 20-40 minutes should be enough to get the texture of the soft serve.
7. After it turns into a soft serve, put it in a loaf pan, smooth it out with the back of a spoon, cover it with foil, and put it in the freezer for 4 to 6 hours or until it sets.

Salted Caramel Sauce:

1. Put the water, syrup, and sugar in a pot with a heavy bottom. Stir the sugar until it melts completely. Then, add the milk-free butter.
2. Keep stirring until the butter melts. Slowly add the cream while stirring all the time.
3. When the water has boiled for about one minute, take the pan off the heat and add the salt. Keep cool until you're ready to use it.
4. Store the sauce in a jar that won't let air in the fridge. It will stay good for up to two weeks.

73. STRAWBERRY ICE CREAM

Prep Time: 20 Minutes | Cook Time: 00 Minutes

Total Time: 20 Minutes | Serving: 12

Ingredients

- 2 cups of heavy cream
- 1/2 tsp vanilla extract
- 1 cup of whole milk
- 1 cup of sugar
- 2 cups of chopped strawberries
- 1 dash salt

Instructions

1. For the night, the bowl of a 2QT ice cream maker needs to be frozen.
2. Strawberry chunks and 1/2 cup of sugar should be mixed in a medium-sized bowl. Set aside 15 minutes to let the strawberries' juices come out.
3. Make strawberry juice in a blender or food processor.
4. Mix the strawberry mixture with the heavy cream, whole milk, vanilla extract, salt, and sugar in a large bowl. Put away.
5. Pour the strawberry cream mixture into an ice cream maker set up. Follow the manufacturer's instructions and let it run.
6. Now is the time for soft-serve ice cream.
7. Put ice cream into a bread loaf pan and cover it with plastic wrap. This will make ice cream that can be scooped. Freeze for at least six hours or overnight.

74. MANGO COCONUT ICE CREAM

Prep Time: 10 Minutes | Cook Time: 00 Minutes

Total Time: 10 Minutes | Serving: 3

Ingredients

- 2 cups of ripe mango
- 14 ounce can of coconut milk
- ½ cup of sugar

Instructions

1. Combine everything with a blender or food processor.
2. Mix until smooth
3. Put the mango mix into the ice cream maker's bowl. Freeze for about 40 minutes until the texture is like a soft serve.
4. To make it firmer, put it in a container that won't let air in and freeze it for an hour. You can then serve it right away.

75. RASPBERRY ICE CREAM

Prep Time: 10 Minutes | Cook Time: 00 Minutes

Total Time: 10 Minutes | Serving: 12

Ingredients

- 1 cup of white sugar
- 1 tsp vanilla extract
- 2 cup of raspberries
- 2 cups of heavy cream
- 1 cup of whole milk

Instructions

1. Put the sugar and raspberries in a medium-sized bowl and mix them. Leave them alone for 15 minutes to let the raspberry juices out. Put them in a blender and blend them until they are smooth.
2. Put the raspberry sugar mix, heavy cream, milk, and vanilla extract in a large bowl. Use a whisk to stir the ingredients together.
3. Put the ice cream maker on and mix it while running. Follow the manufacturer's instructions and let it run.
4. Now is the time to serve the soft-serve ice cream.
5. In a bread loaf pan, put the ready-made ice cream. Put plastic wrap over it and freeze it for at least six hours or overnight.

76. PINEAPPLE COCONUT ICE CREAM

Prep Time: 15 Minutes | Cook Time: 25 Minutes

Total Time: 40 Minutes | Serving: 10

Ingredients

- 1 1/2 cups of whipping cream
- 1/2 cup of sugar
- 1/2 cup of crushed pineapple
- 1 cup of coconut milk

Instructions

1. Mix the sugar and coconut with a whisk or a fork to remove it.
2. Place in the heavy cream and mix it in.
3. Mix the crushed pineapple well after adding it.
4. Add the pineapple and coconut to the ice cream maker.
5. For about 20 to 25 minutes or as directed by the manufacturer.
6. Hope you enjoy this frozen dessert with pineapple and coconut!

77. COCONUT PINEAPPLE ICE CREAM

Prep Time: 15 Minutes | Cook Time: 00 Minutes

Total Time: 15 Minutes | Serving: 8

Ingredients
- 8 ounces pineapple bits
- 1 ½ cups of half-and-half cream
- 1 cup of flaked coconut toasted
- 1 cups of milk
- 14 ounce Cream of Coconut

Instructions
1. Put the coconut cream and milk in your blender and blend them well.
2. After that, add the cream and stir.
3. Add the pineapple and toasted coconut and mix well.
4. Put everything into the ice cream maker's container and follow the manufacturer's instructions.

78. PINEAPPLE COCONUT ICE CREAM

Prep Time: 20 Minutes | Cook Time: 30 Minutes

Total Time: 50 Minutes | Serving: 12

Ingredients
- 1 tsp coconut extract
- 1 can coconut milk
- ⅓ cup of shredded coconut
- 8 ounces crushed pineapple
- 1 cup of granulated sugar
- 1 ½ cups of heavy cream

Instructions
1. In a large bowl, beat the sugar and coconut milk with an electric mixer until the sugar is gone. After that, add the rest of the ingredients and stir them in.
2. Place the ingredients into an ice cream maker insert that has already been chilled. Churn for 30 minutes.
3. Put the ice cream in a container, tighten the lid, and freeze for two to four hours.

79. CHERRY CHIP ICE CREAM

Prep Time: 10 Minutes | Cook Time: 00 Minutes

Total Time: 10 Minutes | Serving: 12

Ingredients

For the Cherry Ice Cream:

- 1/4 tsp almond extract
- 2 cups of heavy whipping cream
- 1/4 tsp vanilla extract
- 2/3 cup of granulated sugar
- 1 dash salt
- 2 cups of cherries
- 1 cup of whole milk

For Mixing in:

- 3/4 cup of chocolate chips
- 3/4 cup of cherries
- 2 TBS granulated sugar

Instructions

1. First, freeze the bowl of a 2QT ice cream maker for at least 12 hours. Then, make the ice cream.
2. Put the granulated sugar and 2 cups of the chopped cherries in a large bowl and mix them. Wait about 10 minutes.
3. Put the cherries, sugar, and heavy cream into a blender. Blend until the heavy cream is smooth and the cherries are broken up.
4. Add the milk and mix it into the cream. The salt, vanilla, and almond extract should all be added now.
5. Staining the cherry cream mixture is best to eliminate the cherry skins.
6. After setting up the ice cream maker, put the ice cream in it and churn it for about 30 minutes, following the guide on the maker.
7. Put the last 3/4 cup of cherries and the granulated sugar in a small bowl. Leave it there while you make the ice cream.
8. For more juice, put the cherries through a fine mesh strainer. Make small blots with a paper towel.
9. When the ice cream gets thick enough to be like soft serve, add the chocolate chips and cherry pieces that have been chopped up. For another 5 to 10 minutes, churn it until they are well mixed in.
10. Put the ice cream in a 2QT container, cover it, and freeze for at least 6 hours, or even better, overnight. If you want it creamy and soft, serve it right away.

80. BLACKBERRY ICE CREAM

Prep Time: 25 Minutes | Cook Time: 5 Minutes

Total Time: 30 Minutes | Serving: 10

Ingredients

For the Blackberry Sauce Swirl:

- 3 TBS granulated sugar
- 1 tsp cornstarch
- 1 cup of blackberries

For the Blackberry Ice Cream:

- 1 cup of whole milk
- 1 cup of granulated sugar
- 1 1/2 cups of blackberries
- 1 pinch salt
- 1/2 tsp vanilla extract
- 2 cups of heavy cream

Instructions

For the Blackberry Sauce Swirl:

1. Place the cornstarch, sugar, and blackberries in a small saucepan. After 5 minutes of stirring and mashing the berries over medium-low heat, the sauce should thicken.
2. This sauce should be put in a small bowl and in the fridge to cool down until needed.

For the Blackberry Ice Cream:

1. Put the blackberries and sugar in a medium-sized bowl. Mix the ingredients and mash the blackberries a bit. Wait 15 minutes, and then do it.
2. Combine the sugar and blackberries in a blender or food processor. Strain the berry mix to get the blackberry seeds out of it.
3. Mix the blackberry and sugar mixture pureed in a large bowl with the heavy cream, milk, vanilla, and salt.
4. Put the mix in a machine already set up, and it says on the box, or let it run for 30 minutes until the ice cream gets thicker.
5. Put blackberry ice cream scoops into a 2-quart container. Then, drizzle blackberry sauce over the top. Add more ice cream and sauce until the container is full and the ice cream is gone.
6. Lock the ice cream container shut and put it in the freezer for at least six hours or overnight for firmer ice cream.

81. WATERMELON ICE CREAM

Prep Time: 15 Minutes | Cook Time: 25 Minutes

Total Time: 40 Minutes | Serving: 10

Ingredients

Watermelon:

- ➢ 2 1/2-3 cups of watermelon
- ➢ 1/4 cup of sugar

Ice Cream Base:

- ➢ 2 cups of heavy cream
- ➢ 1/2 cup of milk
- ➢ 1 tsp vanilla extract
- ➢ 1/2 cup of chocolate chips
- ➢ 1 envelope gelatin
- ➢ 1/2 cup of sugar
- ➢ 1/4 tsp salt

Instructions

Watermelon:

1. In a bowl, blend watermelon and add 1/4 cup of sugar.
2. Put 1 1/2 cups of watermelon puree in a small saucepan and set it over medium-low heat.
3. Bring the watermelon puree to a boil and keep it going.
4. Keep the watermelon mix in the fridge for about three hours or until it is completely cool.

Ice Cream Base:

1. Mix milk and sugar with a hand mixer or whisk until the sugar is gone.
2. Mix the cooled watermelon puree into the milk.
3. Add the cream, vanilla, and salt, and sprinkle the gelatin. Make sure the gelatin dissolves all the way. Use an ice cream maker to make it.
4. About 20 to 25 minutes to mix.
5. When the ice cream is being made, add chocolate chips.
6. Allow the ice cream maker to mix for five more minutes.
7. Have fun with this tasty summer treat!

82. KIWI FRUIT ICE CREAM

Prep Time: 10 Minutes | Cook Time: 00 Minutes

Total Time: 10 Minutes | Serving: 4

Ingredients

- 4 kiwi fruit
- 100 ml milk
- 2 tbsp icing sugar
- 150 ml double cream

Instructions

1. First, peel and cut up the kiwis. A stick blender can mix the milk and icing sugar. Use a food processor instead.
2. Double cream should be added and mixed in. See if it tastes sweet.
3. If it needs it, add more icing sugar.
4. Follow the machine's instructions after putting the mix in an ice cream maker. When it's done, put it in the freezer.

83. KEY LIME PIE ICE CREAM

Prep Time: 10 Minutes | Cook Time: 00 Minutes

Total Time: 10 Minutes | Serving: 6

Ingredients

For the Key Lime Ice Cream:

- Zest of 1 Lime
- 6 Graham Crackers
- 1/2 cup of Key Lime Juice
- 1 can of Sweetened Condensed Milk
- Dash of Salt
- 1 1/2 cups of Whole Milk
- 1/2 cup of Heavy Cream

Ice Cream Garnishes:

- Key Lime Wedges
- Graham Cracker Pieces

Instructions

1. Add milk, lime juice, heavy cream, salt, and sweetened condensed milk to a large bowl. Use a whisk to mix the ingredients.
2. Insert a lid or plastic wrap with the ice cream base over the bowl. Put the bowl in the fridge for at least 4 hours or overnight. Though not necessary, it is suggested.
3. After the key lime ice cream mixture has been chilled, put it in your ice cream maker and churn it according to the machine's directions.
4. Mix 1/3 cup of graham crackers into the ice cream after churning it. Next, put the ice cream into a container in the freezer. Cover it and put it in the freezer for an hour or until it's firm. Add one tsp of graham crackers to each serving.
5. Add lime wedges as a decoration.

84. BANANA PUDDING ICE CREAM

Prep Time: 10 Minutes | Cook Time: 00 Minutes

Total Time: 10 Minutes | Serving: 8

Ingredients

- 1/2 cup of white sugar
- 2 eggs
- 1/2 cup of packed brown sugar
- 1/8 tsp salt
- 2 very ripe bananas
- 1 1/2 tsp vanilla extract
- 1 cup of crushed Nilla wafers
- 1 1/2 cups of half and half
- 1 cup of heavy whipping cream

Instructions

1. Using medium-low heat, melt the butter in a saucepan. Include the salt and brown sugar. Just keep stirring for five minutes or until the sugar is gone.
2. Take the pan off the heat. Get an LD bowl and add eggs to it. Slowly add about half of the sugar mixture to the eggs while whisking.
3. Put the egg mixture in the saucepan, and the half-and-half remains.
4. Add the cream and stir. Mix it over medium-low heat until it gets thick enough to stick to a spoon. A short time to a long time.
5. Take the pan off the heat and add the vanilla extract. Put the mix through a sieve with a fine mesh into a bowl. Let it cool to room temperature.
6. If you want to make ice cream, mix in mashed banana after it has cooled down. Follow the directions on the package to freeze. About 5 minutes before the time is up, add the Nilla wafers.
7. Put the ice cream in the freezer for about an hour if it's still too soft for your taste.

85. ORANGE ICE CREAM

Prep Time: 15 Minutes | Cook Time: 25 Minutes

Total Time: 40 Minutes | Serving: 10

Ingredients

- 1 1/2 cups of heavy whipping cream
- 1 1/2 cups of orange juice
- 1 tsp vanilla extract
- 1/3 cup of sugar
- 1/2 cup of shaved chocolate
- 1 tbsp orange zest
- 1 tbsp lemon juice

Instructions

1. Mix all the ingredients in a large bowl by stirring them around until the sugar is gone.
2. Put the ice cream mix into your machine and mix it as the maker tells you to.
3. Churn for about 25 minutes or as directed by the manufacturer.
4. If you want, you can add shaved chocolate in the last 5 minutes of mixing.
5. Have fun with your tasty treat

86. BERRY RIPPLE ICE CREAM

Prep Time: 10 Minutes | Cook Time: 00 Minutes

Total Time: 10 Minutes | Serving: 12

Ingredients

- Juice 1 lemon
- 600ml Carton whipping cream
- 200g Carnation Fat-Free Condensed Milk
- 55g Caster sugar
- 400g Fresh or frozen berries
- 1tbsp Vanilla extract

Instructions

1. Let the sugar and lemon juice cook with the berries in a pan until the mixture is half as much as before. Pour it through a sieve to remove the seeds after it cools down.
2. While whipping, the cream should get soft peaks. Add the vanilla and sweetened condensed milk next, and whip it for a short time more. Mix the berry sauce into the ice cream with a spoon in a container that can be frozen. The food will be solid while it's frozen.
3. Before putting it in ice cream cones, let it sit at room temperature for 5-10 minutes.

87. APPLE PIE ICE CREAM

Prep Time: 10 Minutes | Cook Time: 15 Minutes

Total Time: 25 Minutes | Serving: 8

Ingredients

- 2 large apples
- 1 tsp cinnamon
- 2 cups of whipping cream
- 1 1/2 cups of half and half
- 3 Tbsp sugar
- 1/2 tsp salt
- 1 1/4 cups of sugar
- 1 1/2 cups of whole milk
- 2 tsp cinnamon
- 1 Tbsp butter
- 5 cinnamon graham crackers
- 1 Tbsp vanilla

Instructions

1. Cut apples into dice after peeling and core them.
2. Add butter and cook the apples. Put in 3 tbsp of sugar and 1 tsp of cinnamon. Cook for 8 to 10 minutes, until the sugar turns brown and caramelizes. Take it out of the pan and let it cool.
3. Break up Graham crackers.
4. To make ice cream, put milk, 1/4 cup of sugar, salt, half-and-half, vanilla extract, whipping cream, and 2 tsp of cinnamon into the machine.
5. Do it until it's done.
6. Add the browned apples and crushed cinnamon graham crackers and mix them in. Place in the freezer to get hard.

88. STRAWBERRY BALSAMIC ICE CREAM

Prep Time: 10 Minutes | Cook Time: 30 Minutes

Total Time: 40 Minutes | Serving: 5

Ingredients

- 2 cups of fresh strawberries
- ⅓ cup of granulated sugar
- ¾ cup of dark brown sugar
- 5 large egg yolks
- 1 ¾ cup of milk
- 2 tbsp vanilla extract
- ¼ cup of balsamic vinegar
- ¼ tsp ground cinnamon
- 2 cup of heavy cream

Instructions

1. Put the egg yolks and sugar in a medium-sized saucepan with a heavy bottom. Whisk them together until they turn a pale yellow colour.
2. Pour the heavy cream, milk, and vanilla extract into the saucepan. Use a whisk to mix the ingredients.
3. Set the heat to medium and whisk it constantly while it boils so it doesn't burn.
4. Lower the heat and keep whisking the ice cream custard until it gets thick enough to stick to a spoon. When you can leave a mark on the back of the spoon after running your finger along it, the custard is done.
5. Take the ice cream custard out of the heat and put it in a bowl or container. Let it cool to room temperature.
6. Once it's at room temperature, put it in the fridge with the balsamic strawberry sauce and cover tightly. Chill for at least 4-5 hours or overnight.
7. If you want to make ice cream, chill the ice cream custard first, follow the maker's instructions and churn it.
8. Once the ice cream is smooth, put half of the vanilla ice cream into a container with a lid. Cover the ice cream with half of the strawberry balsamic sauce.
9. Add the last ice cream to the container and then spread the rest of the strawberry balsamic sauce on top of it.
10. Use a knife to mix the strawberry balsamic sauce into the ice cream. For best results, freeze the dish overnight before serving. Make sure the lid fits tightly on top.
11. It makes about a quart of Strawberry Balsamic Ice Cream.

89. PEANUT BUTTER CHOCOLATE CHUNK ICE CREAM

Prep Time: 10 Minutes | Cook Time: 00 Minutes

Total Time: 10 Minutes | Serving: 8

Ingredients

- 4 ounces semi-sweet chocolate
- 14 ounce can of sweetened condensed milk
- 1/3 cup of creamy peanut butter
- 2 cups of heavy whipping cream
- 2 ounces cream cheese
- 1 tbsp vanilla extract

Instructions

1. Put the sweetened condensed milk, peanut butter, and vanilla into a large bowl and mix them with a whisk.
2. Use an electric mixer to make the cream cheese soft and smooth in a different bowl.
3. Add the heavy cream slowly while beating at medium speed. After adding everything else, beat on high for two to three minutes until thick.
4. Put the whipped cream mixture into the peanut butter mixture two parts at a time, mixing each time until there are no more streaks. If you stir the whipped cream too much, it might lose its air. Add the chopped chocolate slowly.
5. Put the mix into an ice cream tub or a loaf pan. Put a lid or plastic wrap on top. Put in the fridge for at least 6 hours or until it's completely firm.

90. CHOCOLATE CHIP ICE CREAM

Prep Time: 15 Minutes | Cook Time: 25 Minutes

Total Time: 40 Minutes | Serving: 10

Ingredients

- 1 1/2 tsp vanilla
- 3/4 cup of chocolate chips
- 1/2 cup of sugar
- 2 cups of heavy whipping cream
- 1 cup of milk

Instructions

1. Put the sugar in a medium bowl and mix it with a wire whisk or hand mixer on low speed for one to two minutes. This will dissolve the sugar.
2. Put the heavy cream and vanilla and stir slowly.
3. Put the mix into the machine that makes ice cream.
4. Mix for about 20 to 25 minutes or as directed by the manufacturer.
5. Mix chocolate into the ice cream. For another 5 minutes, churn.
6. Have fun with your tasty treat!

91. CHOCOLATE PECAN PIE ICE CREAM

Prep Time: 10 Minutes | Cook Time: 00 Minutes

Total Time: 10 Minutes | Serving: 8

Ingredients

For the ice cream:

- 3 tsp vanilla extract
- 1/2 tsp kosher salt
- 2 cups of heavy cream
- 3/4 cup of sugar
- 1 cup of whole milk

For the mix-ins:

- 1 cup of chopped dark chocolate
- 1 1/4 cups of all-purpose flour
- 1 tbsp brandy
- 1/2 cup of unsalted butter
- 3 tbsp ice water
- 1 tsp salt
- 1/2 cup of dark corn syrup
- 2 eggs
- 1/2 cup of chopped pecans
- 1/4 cup of unsalted butter
- 1 tsp vanilla extract
- 2 tbsp sugar

Instructions

1. First, make the crust for the pie. It is time to heat the oven to 350°F. Melt the butter and put the sugar and salt in a food processor. Then, add the flour and mix it all. Pulse the food processor to make butter pieces about the size of a dime.

2. Drop the ice water into the dough mixture while stirring it in a large bowl. Do this until the dough starts to get wet all over. Using your hands, quickly and gently fold the dough repeatedly, pressing it together. Some parts should be dry, and some should be wet. For a 1/4-inch thickness, roll it out on a lightly floured surface, folding it over on itself if it doesn't stick together well enough. Place the dough in the fridge for 15 minutes before attempting to roll it out if it is too sticky.

3. After putting the dough on a baking sheet lined with parchment paper, poke holes in it all over with a fork and bake for 20 minutes or until it turns golden brown.

4. Let the crust cool while you make the filling and ice cream.

5. You should use a whisk to mix the rest of the mix-in ingredients in a medium saucepan, leaving out the toasted nuts and chopped chocolate. Over medium-low heat, stir the mixture all the time for about 5 minutes or until it gets thick and shiny. Add the pecans and mix them in after taking it off the heat.

6. Make the ice cream: After combining all the ingredients with a whisk, put them in your ice cream maker and freeze them according to the manufacturer's directions.

7. While the ice cream is freezing, break up the baked pie crust into pieces about the size of quarters.

8. Add the pecan filling, chopped chocolate, and crumbled pie crust about 5 minutes before the ice cream hardens. Put the ice cream in a container that can go in the freezer after churning it. Freeze it until it's firm before scooping it out and serving it.

92. CHOCOLATE CHIP COOKIE DOUGH ICE CREAM

Prep Time: 20 Minutes | Cook Time: 25 Minutes

Total Time: 45 Minutes | Serving: 10

Ingredients

Cookie Dough:

- 1/4 cup of sugar
- 1/2 cup of brown sugar
- 1 cup of flour
- 1/2 tsp salt
- 1/2 cup of butter
- 1/2 tsp vanilla

Ice Cream Base:

- 1 1/2 tsp vanilla
- 1/2 cup of chocolate chips
- 1/2 cup of cookie dough
- 1 cup of milk
- 1/2 cup of sugar
- 2 cups of heavy whipping cream

Instructions

Cookie Dough:

1. You can make this dough while the ice cream base is in the maker.
2. Mix the sugars, vanilla, and butter until they are well mixed.
3. Salt and flour.
4. Mix everything well.
5. Make little balls that are about the size of a chocolate chip.
6. They should be manageable, or they will get stuck in what you're making.

Ice Cream Base:

1. Add sugar to milk and stir until the sugar is gone.
2. Put in some heavy cream and vanilla extract.
3. Put the mix into the machine that makes ice cream.
4. Mix in an ice cream maker for 15 to 20 minutes or as the manufacturer directs.
5. Make the cookie dough at the same time.
6. To the ice cream mix, add chocolate chips and cookie dough balls.
7. Pour in the ice cream and mix for five more minutes.

93. CHOCOLATE ALMOND BUTTER ICE CREAM

Prep Time: 25 Minutes | Cook Time: 10 Minutes

Total Time: 35 Minutes | Serving: 10

Ingredients

- ➢ 6 tbsp cacao powder
- ➢ ½ cup of almond butter for swirling
- ➢ 2 13.5ounce cans full-fat coconut milk
- ➢ 1 ½ tsp gelatin
- ➢ ½ cup of honey
- ➢ ½ cup of almond butter

Instructions

1. Ensure the ice cream bowl has been frozen for at least 24 hours before starting.
2. Honey and coconut milk should be put in a small saucepan. While whisking, make sure the mixture is smooth.
3. Cover with gelatin and let it bloom for five minutes.
4. After adding the almond butter and cacao and whisking them in, turn the heat to medium. Cook until warm, but don't let it boil.
5. Pour into a container and put in the fridge for 5 to 8 hours or until cool.
6. Put the cool mixture into your ice cream maker and churn it according to the directions on the box. It took me twenty minutes to make mine.
7. Prepare a loaf pan while the ice cream is being made. Place parchment paper around the edges and trim any extra hanging over.
8. Pour ice cream and almond butter into a layer pan, then freeze until solid. It's best to do this overnight.
9. Or you can eat it right away; it will be like a soft serve.
10. Let it sit at room temperature for 10 minutes to make it easier to scoop.

94. MAPLE-WALNUT ICE CREAM

Prep Time: 20 Minutes | Cook Time: 00 Minutes

Total Time: 20 Minutes | Serving: 6

Ingredients

- 1 egg
- 2 tbsp arrowroot powder
- ⅓ cup of maple syrup
- 1 ½ tsp vanilla extract
- pinch fine Himalayan salt
- ½ cup of walnuts
- 1 can full-fat coconut milk

Instructions

1. Mix the egg, arrowroot powder, salt, and coconut milk in a medium-sized saucepan using a whisk.
2. Heat the mixture over medium-low heat and stir it often until it starts to boil and get thick. While it's still cool, add the vanilla extract and mix well.
3. Let the mixture cool in the fridge overnight.
4. It's time to use your ice cream maker. Put the walnuts and maple syrup into the chilled ice cream custard and mix them in.
5. Put chopped walnuts and maple syrup on top of the dish.

95. CHOCOLATE COOKIE ICE CREAM

Prep Time: 15 Minutes | Cook Time: 25 Minutes

Total Time: 40 Minutes | Serving: 10

Ingredients

- 3/4 cup of cookies
- 1/2 cup of sugar
- 1 cup of milk
- 1 tsp vanilla
- 2 cups of heavy cream
- 1 1/3 cup of chocolate

Instructions

1. Use the stove or microwave to warm the milk until it bubbles around the edges.
2. Make small pieces of chocolate in a blender or food processor while you wait.
3. Mix sugar and chocolate.
4. Once the chocolate is smooth, add the hot milk and stir them together.
5. Give this some time to cool down.
6. After the mix has cooled down, add the heavy cream and vanilla.
7. Put in the fridge for at least 30 minutes.
8. Put the mix into the ice cream maker.
9. For about 20 to 25 minutes or as directed by the manufacturer.
10. Combine cookie crumbs with chocolate ice cream.
11. Churn for five more minutes. Yummy!

96. CHOCOLATE PEANUT BUTTER ICE CREAM

Prep Time: 10 Minutes | Cook Time: 00 Minutes

Total Time: 10 Minutes | Serving: 4

Ingredients

- ➢ pinch coarse sea salt
- ➢ 1 ½ cups of whole milk
- ➢ ¾ cup of granulated sugar
- ➢ 1 tsp vanilla extract
- ➢ 2 cups of heavy cream
- ➢ ¼ cup of hot fudge
- ➢ 1 bag miniature peanut butter cups
- ➢ ½ cup of peanut butter
- ➢ ⅔ cup of cocoa powder

Instructions

1. You can freeze the ice cream maker container ahead of time if you need to.
2. Mix the milk, cream, sugar, cocoa powder, extract, and salt with a whisk until the mixture looks like chocolate milk. Incorporating the cocoa powder might take a while. Put the mix in the fridge for at least 30 minutes.
3. After stirring the milk mixture again, pour it into the ice cream maker set-up. Churn for 30 to 40 minutes, or until the texture of soft serve. This will depend on your model.
4. Put the peanut butter in the ice cream. It's almost done. Melt it in the microwave for 20 seconds. It will be simple to mix in.
5. Immediately mix the peanut butter cups into the ice cream that has been churned. Place half of the ice cream in a large container that can go in the freezer.
6. Divide the hot fudge and peanut butter in half. Add them to the ice cream and mix them using a knife. Add more ice cream and toppings, and do it again. Cover the top with wax paper, then put the lid on top. Freeze for three to four hours or until the food is hard.

97. ALMOND MILK ICE CREAM

Prep Time: 5 Minutes | Cook Time: 25 Minutes

Total Time: 30 Minutes | Serving: 10

Ingredients
- 4 cups of almond milk
- 1 tsp vanilla extract
- 5 tbsp sugar

Instructions

1. Mix sugar and vanilla into almond milk until the sugar is completely mixed in. After 40 seconds, stir the food in the microwave.
2. For 25 minutes, or until it gets thick, put the stir in an ice cream maker and run it. Anytime, or freeze it for later use.

98. FRUITY PEBBLES ICE CREAM

Prep Time: 10 Minutes | Cook Time: 5 Minutes

Total Time: 15 Minutes | Serving: 8

Ingredients
- 3 egg yolks
- 2 cups of whole milk
- 1.5 cups of heavy cream
- 2 cups of fruity pebbles
- ⅓ cup of sugar

Instructions

1. Put the milk in a small saucepan and heat it until it boils. After turning off the heat, add the cereal. Infuse for 10 minutes.
2. With a fine mesh sieve, separate the cereal from the milk. Throw away the soft cereal.
3. Put everything into a blender. Make a smooth mixture.
4. The ice cream base must be in the fridge for at least two hours.
5. Put it in an ice cream machine. Churn according to the directions on the package, as soft serve right away, or put in a freezer container and freeze until it's firm enough to scoop.

99. MARSHMALLOW SWIRL ICE CREAM

Prep Time: 10 Minutes | Cook Time: 00 Minutes | Total Time: 10 Minutes | Serving: 16

Ingredients

Ice cream base:

- 2 cups of milk
- 4 large egg yolks
- 1/4 tsp xanthan gum
- 1/2 cup of granulated sugar
- 2 cups of heavy cream
- 1 tbsp Pure Vanilla Extract

Marshmallow swirl:

- 1 tsp Pure Vanilla Extract
- 3 large egg whites
- 1/3 cup of water
- 3/4 cup of light corn syrup
- 1/2 tsp cream of tartar
- 3/4 cup of granulated sugar

Instructions

1. To make the ice cream base, Put the cream and milk in a saucepan and set it over medium-high heat. Put the pan on low heat, add the vanilla, and wait 30 minutes.
2. Separately, beat the egg yolks, sugar, and xanthan gum in a different saucepan until they are fluffy and light. The warm milk and cream should be mixed into the egg yolk mix.
3. Put the pan on low heat and stir the mixture until it gets thicker. It will show up as 170°F to 180°F on a digital thermometer. To make the custard cool, take it off the heat and leave it alone. A skin won't form if you stir it every so often. Put it in the fridge with the lid on for at least two hours or all night.
4. To mix the marshmallows, Add the cream of tartar and egg whites to the bowl of an electric mixer with a whisk attachment. Set the bowl aside.
5. Put the water, sugar, corn syrup or honey in a medium saucepan. Do a stir to mix. Set a candy thermometer in the mixture and heat it over medium-high heat. Refrain from stirring it as it cooks, or it will get grainy.
6. While the sugar syrup is bubbling and the thermometer reads about 225°F, begin beating the egg whites until they form soft peaks. A sugar syrup at 240°F should be in the pan when the egg whites are done. The syrup needs to be taken off the heat. Pour the syrup into the egg whites slowly down the side of the bowl while the mixer is on medium-low speed. The stream should be thin and steady.
7. At first, the whites will lose some air, but keep beating them, and the mixture will rise again. Spread should be thick and shiny after 7 to 8 minutes of whipping. Another minute of whipping after adding the vanilla. Place the spread in a jar that won't let air in and leave it at room temperature.
8. Put the cold custard into an ice cream maker and freeze it as the machine tells you to. Mix in 1 1/2 cups of marshmallow spread to see it in the batter. Grow stronger while it's still soft.
9. If you want to keep the ice cream for up to two months, put it in a container with a lid that fits tightly on top.

100. ROCKY ROAD ICE CREAM

Prep Time: 15 Minutes | Cook Time: 00 Minutes

Total Time: 15 Minutes | Serving: 8

Ingredients

- 1½ cups of whole milk
- 1 cup of mini marshmallows
- 1½ cups of heavy whipping cream
- 4 egg yolks
- 1 cup of granulated sugar
- ¼ cup of unsweetened cocoa powder
- ½ cup of mini chocolate chips
- 1 tbsp vanilla extract
- ½ cup of chopped walnuts

Instructions

1. Follow the directions on how to freeze the ice cream maker bowl.
2. Mix cream, milk, sugar, egg yolks, and cocoa in a large saucepan with a whisk until the mixture is smooth.
3. Put the liquid in the pan and stir it on medium heat until it separates. It's a little thicker, but not like pudding. Combine vanilla and mix it in. You can taste it and change how sweet it is.
4. Put it in a big bowl or measuring cup made of glass. Put a piece of plastic wrap on top to keep skin from forming.
5. Put in the fridge until it's completely cold.
6. Put it in the ice cream maker and churn it for 20 minutes or until it's the consistency of soft serve. Take the last five minutes and add the nuts, chocolate chips, and marshmallows. You can churn the mixture or stir it in by hand.
7. Put the mixture into a baking dish or glass loaf pan and freeze for 4 to 6 hours or until it is firm.
8. Let it sit for 5 to 10 minutes at room temperature before serving. Wrap extra food in plastic wrap and freeze for up to three months.

101. CHOCOLATE BROWNIE ICE CREAM

Prep Time: 30 Minutes | Cook Time: 00 Minutes

Total Time: 30 Minutes | Serving: 6

Ingredients

- 1 cup of brownie bits
- 1½ cups of heavy cream
- pinch salt
- 2 tsp vanilla
- ¾ cup of sugar
- 1½ cups of half and half
- ½ cup of unsweetened cocoa powder

Instructions

1. In a bowl, put cocoa powder.
2. Pour in ¼ cup of half-and-half and mix it well until it's all mixed in. Add one more quarter cup and keep stirring. There should be a lot of chocolate in the mix. Make sure that all of the cocoa powder is mixed in. There shouldn't be any dry cocoa powder.
3. While stirring well, slowly add the rest of the half-and-half. When you add the liquid, stir it well with a whisk. This keeps any small lumps from forming.
4. Put in some salt, vanilla, and sugar.
5. Add heavy cream and mix.
6. Place the ice cream mix in the frozen bowl of an automatic ice cream maker. Churn the ice cream for twenty to twenty-five minutes or until it forms. Like soft serve ice cream, it will be thick.
7. Put ice cream in a container in the freezer and top it with brownie bits. Lightly stir to spread out the brownie pieces.
8. Put it in the freezer for two to four hours before serving.

Made in the USA
Monee, IL
17 November 2024

70342890R00050